Alternate Realities

Alternate Realities

The Search for the
Full Human Being

Lawrence LeShan

M. EVANS AND COMPANY, INC. / NEW YORK, N.Y.   10017

M. Evans and Company titles are distributed in
the United States by the J.B. Lippincott Company,
East Washington Square, Philadelphia, Pa. 19105;
and in Canada by McClelland & Stewart Ltd.,
25 Hollinger Road, Toronto M4B 3G2, Ontario

LIBRARY OF CONGRESS CATALOGING IN PUBLICATION DATA
LeShan, Lawrence L   1920-
   Alternate realities.

   Includes bibliographical references.
   1. Psychical research.   2 Reality.   I. Title.
BF1031.L42 1976   133.8'01   76-14488
ISBN 0-87131-217-4

Design by Joel Schick

Manufactured in the United States of America

9 8 7 6 5 4 3 2 1

*To My Mother Rose V. Rosenbaum
who started me on the search
for the meaning of reality*

Contents

Introduction

In the beginning of my last book on the relationships of man and reality (*The Medium, The Mystic and the Physicist: Towards a General Theory of the Paranormal*[1]), I offered a quotation from Plato. To illustrate my attitude toward the present book, I would like to repeat it here:

> 'I would not,' says Socrates, 'be confident in everything I say about the argument: but one thing I would fight for to the end, both in word or deed if I were able—that if we believed we should try to find out what is not known, we should be better and braver and less idle than if we believed that what we do not know it is impossible to find out and that we need not even try.'
>
> —THE MENO

This book is a "work in progress." Much of it is open to dispute and I hope that the undoubted errors in the formulation of the basic thesis will be corrected as time goes on. As a matter of fact, I hope to see more clearly myself in the future and be one of the correctors.

The central idea of this book is that we human beings invent reality as much as we discover it, and that if this is comprehended, we have a wide choice as to how we invent it and therefore, what sort of world we live in. There are, the thesis continues, a number of basically different, valid ways of organizing whatever is "out there," and we can choose from among these the one that will satisfy our needs and advance us toward our goals at the moment. Many of our personal and interpersonal problems seem to arise from using the wrong method of construing reality to accomplish a particular task, or from mixing two or more methods without being aware of what we are doing. This thesis also seems to provide an acceptable and useful solution to the "impossible paradox" of ESP, and to the problems of "survival" of the personality after biological death and of the existence or nonexistence of spirit entities.

This set of concepts appears to me to be a logical and inexorable next step in the "revolution of thought" that started with Immanuel Kant and is still continuing in philosophy, art, and literature to basically affect our culture. I owe especially heavy debts for whatever is of value in this book to the philosophers Ernst Cassirer and Morris Raphael Cohen and to the physicist-philosopher Henry Margenau. Dr. Margenau has been kind enough to give me much positive encouragement as well as a great deal of constructive criticism. I am not at all sure, however, how happily Cassirer or Cohen would regard where I have taken their ideas. In any case, whatever their response to the specific direction that I have tried to take their "revolution," I am sure that they would agree on the necessity to continue it.

Since writing this book, I have read Jacob Needleman's beautiful *A Sense of the Cosmos* (Doubleday, 1976). In some way, his book and this are complementary. I cannot really decide whether my book should serve as an introduction to his or vice versa!

I could not have written *Alternate Realities* without the continual support and encouragement of James S. McDonnell, who has my heartfelt gratitude for giving me the time to work at it and for his cogent criticisms. I also gladly express my thanks to Arthur Twitchell, Colin Wilson, Anne Appelbaum, Henry Margenau, Robert Laidlaw, Edgar Jackson, Rosalind Heywood, Jacob Needleman, Elizabeth Sewell, Michael Witunski, and Eda LeShan for their repeated reading of various drafts of the manuscript and the benefit of their comments.

There is so much to learn about the reality we are, make, and live in. Perhaps the poet Yeats was right when he wrote, "Man can embody truth, but he cannot know it." It is, however, our task and glory as human beings to try to do both. This book is one, small, stumbling attempt.

Alternate Realities

Whatever the advances of science may do for the universe, there is one thing that they have never yet done and show no prospect of doing—namely, to make it less marvelous.

F. W. H. MYERS

The physicist does not discover, he creates his universe.

—HENRY MARGENAU

Reality is emotional, intellectual, psychological and spiritual as well as physical, but try explaining that to a goldfish.

—JUDITH VIORST

Poems are made by fools like me,
But only God can make a tree;

And only God who makes the tree
Also makes the fools like me.

But only fools like me, you see,
Can make a God, who makes a tree.

—E. Y. HARBURG

Where Did the Melody Come From?

We have always known that there was something wrong. Behind our busyness, behind the working at and worrying about our everyday life and our survival from year to year, were the questions: "What does it mean?" "Why are we here and where is here?" "Why do we love, fear, hate, kill, protect ourselves, die?" "Do we have any real choices? If so, what are they?" "What does being born mean?" "What does dying mean?" "What is love?" "Is there more to the world than we can see?" Behind our constant activity and our concern about our activities and plans there lies a dim unease about these questions and our lack of any answers of which we can be sure.

We certainly today do not have answers to these questions. As much as at any time in history we are still in the grip of our daily life and reacting to its events with most of our concentration and energy. But something new has been added. We now have a new concept, a new tool we can work with that seems to offer a promise of helping us toward more understandings of the great problems: What is man? Is the universe friendly?

It is, of course, not a new tool in the sense that it has never been hinted at before. It has been stated many times in many ways by the great explorers of "what is" of our race. But now, perhaps, we can begin to grasp it and to examine ourselves and the universe with it.

The tool—for what is a concept but a tool?[2]—is basically simple, and because it is simple it is exceedingly hard to grasp. It also flies directly in the face of everything we have been taught to believe in and upon which we have built our life and our society. It seems, therefore, completely opposed to common sense, to "reality," to the solid foundations of "what is." We tend to reject it before we have begun to listen to it. "The foundations of reality and of our knowledge are firm and we know them," we say. "An idea that goes against them is rubbish."

But *are* the foundations firm? If they were would we not know the answers to the great questions instead of forever ignoring them, running from them, or anxiously pretending we know the answers? Would we not—if they *were* firm—feel secure and strong in our innermost beings as we stood on the rock of known truth about the nature of ourselves and our world? Would we not then stand together as human in a shared, known knowledge of the nature of man, stand together in agreement on the great questions as we do on the trivial ones? We well know how to reach agreement on how to do small things—make ink or typewriters, or travel to Chicago—but have not apparently the faintest notion of how to reach agreement on the great things: the nature of a human being or where he belongs in the universe or what he owes to his neighbor and what he owes to himself. Nor even are we able to be completely clear on the meaning of the terms "neighbor" and "self."

No, the foundations are not firm, no matter how energetic we are in avoiding looking at them or in our pretense that we know the meaning of our own life. At best we can say to ourselves, "This I will act as if I believe. This I will give my life to, hoping it is truth. This I will have faith in."

It is part of our greatness that we have been able to go on without a solid base of knowledge; that, heroically, we have been able to make our lives as much as we have, that we could progress this far from the caves, and that we could stay alive with the great questions unanswered; that, aware we are alive and knowing we must die and not knowing what that means, we could go on living. This is a measure of our strength and resources as human beings. Now perhaps we can go a little bit further, a step forward in finding ourselves and our meaning.

What is this new tool for understanding that seems to hold such a promise? It is that what we see and hear around us is at least as much our invention as it is our discovery; that we contribute so much to the existence of the reality of the world we know that we can never separate what we create from what is already "out there." From this the next step inexorably follows: There are other ways of creating our contribution to what is real and thereby changing reality. The next step is even harder: We each have a responsibility for creating and maintaining the universe we live in; what the world is like is to a large—and as yet unknown—degree up to us.

The idea seems ridiculous at first thought. It seems crazy and, at best, a course to a complete chaos, a madhouse of a universe. Common sense says it is madness. Everything we have learned about reality and how to function, to get along, in the world leads us to reject it out of hand. And yet, if our everyday view of the world is sound, why do we not yet know clearly what we can know, what we ought to do, what we dare hope?[3] Why has it led us into the impossible situation where we must spend our lives avoiding such questions? Why can music or art or sometimes a simple scene on television thrill us, bring tears to our eyes or hope to our hearts? Why can we not figure out a way to stop killing each other? Why have the students of the human mind and culture never been able to tell us what love is, what the self is, what death is? Each of us may cling to one or another answer to these questions, but we are well aware that many other people, including many we respect and admire, do not agree with us. If we let ourselves wonder at this—as we rarely do—we are troubled by it and know for a moment how weak are the foundations of our knowledge.

So the answer that comes immediately to mind—that this new concept flies in the face of common sense—has no strength; there is no common sense about the big questions, only about the small ones. For the big questions we only share an agreement not to discuss them or look at them, and in this agreement we pretend to ourselves that we have a firm, shared basis of agreement on the answers, when all we have is an unspoken pact to evade them because they make us too uncomfortable.

The new concept starts with the knowledge that we have always believed that there is a firm, unalterable reality "out there," and the human task was to discover what it is, what things are in it, what laws govern it. We—we humans—sat within our bodies and observed, tried out different ways of doing things, found out what happened when we did, and learned new ways of accomplishing our goals. We learned to cut a log into segments and make wheels, and with more trying, to grease the wheels, and later to have them roll on ball bearings. We learned how to boil surgical instruments to prevent infection, and to bend light through lenses so that we could observe the bacteria that were the sources of the infection. We learned many things and ways of doing things of great value, but as long as we were limited by our basic idea—that things "out there" were as they were—we could only learn about the small questions, never about the big ones. We could not learn about love and death, about the nature of self and others, about what a human being is and how he is related to the universe.

Sometimes, to make progress past a certain point, we have to change the basic way we think about it; to have a revolution of thought. If we can make no more progress considering the earth as the center of the solar system, a center about which the other planets and the sun revolve, we find we can go further if we change the very basis of our search. We go on only by changing to the idea of the sun as the center about which the other planets, *and* earth, revolve. It is to some such task and revolution we are called now.[4] The new concept is that a human being does not *discover* what is out there, but—to a large degree—creates and maintains it, that he is the organizer of, and responsible for, the reality in which he lives. How large a degree of this reality he creates and maintains, we do not yet know but it is a very major part.

There are two sets of ways in which we are informed that a thought system, an idea as to what reality "is," is no longer very useful, no longer working well. Both appear gradually and mount up until we are forced to bring to use a new way of setting a basis to the thinking we use to solve our problems.

The first is when new problems appear that we know we must solve and that we cannot find solutions to, no matter how hard we try. Gradually, through failure after failure, it becomes apparent that the old system of organizing reality is not applicable to these problems. If weapons mount up and we must stop killing each other before all of us perish, we seriously begin to try to find ways to do this. If it becomes clear that we are poisoning our only planet to a point at which it will soon become uninhabitable, we try to stop. If it becomes clear that our population is mounting to the point of disaster, we try to stop. With each of these problems, we have seriously been trying and failing. Slowly it is becoming obvious to all of us that our system of describing reality—upon which rests our ability to solve problems—is not adequate to the new tasks. We need a new system. The old one worked fine for yesterday's problems, but does not work for those we face now.

The second set of ways in which we are informed that a change is imminent are the small discrepancies, the little things that do not fit in, that tell us there is something wrong with a large system of explanation. These discrepancies are not important in themselves—we can always adapt to them, individually argue them away—but they are the clues, the signposts that tell us something is not right, that the system of explanation does not quite fit reality. We can generally hammer out some more or less satisfactory explanation for them, but as the discrepancies mount up these become more and more awkward and burdensome, heavier and heavier to carry along. Let us take some trivia of this sort. We judge the shape of an object by its image on our retina. Fine, but turn a coin so it is at an angle to you, halfway between the round side facing you and the flat edge facing you. The image that now falls on your retina is far from a circle; it is a flattened oval, an ellipse. But the coin still looks round. Look at the moon when it is rising and when it is high overhead. Its size, as judged by an astronomer, has not changed, nor has its distance from us. Yet, when rising, it clearly looks four times larger than when it is directly above us. Or, let us consider another trivial example. We judge whether an object is black, gray, or white by the amount of light reflected from it. In sunlight, look at a piece of coal and a sheet of writing paper. The paper looks white, the coal black. Look at the same piece of paper by moonlight when the amount of light it reflects is less than the coal reflected in the daytime. The paper still looks white. Or, consider how we make classes of things. "Surely," we say, "we do not *create* classes. We take them as we find them 'out there,' male and female; animal, vegetable, and mineral; fruit, meat, and vegetable. We are not creating anything; we are observing things and learning their relationships." Why then, asked one philosopher, has no one made a class of red, juicy, edible things and included meat and cherries in it?[5] Or, a class of tall, dark-haired men and women with no earlobes? These are logical classes, but ones we know we would never make. But why not? It becomes clear, as we look at these trivial points, that—at least in some cases—we help cre-ate and maintain the reality we perceive and react to.

When Charles Darwin sailed on the ship, the *Beagle,* to Patagonia, the ship anchored a quarter-mile offshore. Darwin and others rowed ashore in small boats. The natives, a tough, able group who could live in the inhospitable climate of Patagonia where Darwin, you, or I would quickly perish, could see the small boats, but could not see the large sailing ship that was in plain sight to Darwin and the crew.

A group of artists begin to paint in a new way. No one can understand what they are doing or why. For years they continue and no one will look at or buy their pictures. Suddenly, a few people begin to see their paintings as they do and the "beauty" and "greatness" in a van Gogh, a Gauguin, appears. Was it always there? Did we just begin to see it? Or, did we begin to organize and maintain the "reality" of these paintings in a new way? Or, did we begin to perceive and react to the world in a new way and they were the first to do so? What do all these questions mean?

Would you like to watch yourself creating reality? There is an old, simple method to gain a glimpse of yourself doing this. Take a stick with a knob on the end something like a walking stick. Hold it straight out in front of your right eye. Close your left eye. Looking straight ahead, slowly move the walking stick in an arc to the right. There is a spot on the retina known as the "blind spot" that does not have receptors for vision. Soon the knob will be in front of it and you cannot see it. It becomes invisible to you. Since, however, you invent reality as much as you discover it, and the notion of a blank "hole" in the space you observe does not fit into your ideas as to what is "out there," you will not leave a blank space where the knob is. Watch—still looking straight ahead— as you fill in the hole. The edges grow together to fit the background. Whatever colors, lines, etc., are in the background complete themselves to fill in the hole. Shortly it is not there any more; you have created the "natural, logical" pattern to fill it in.

The "fill-in" may not be right, as judged later by examining the wall with both eyes. You are not really seeing the background. It is just the way you imagine the black spot would be filled in from the way you see the rest of the background. But it is so "real" that you cannot tell where the background you "see" in the ordinary way ends and the background you have invented begins. And so strong is your habit of creating reality that even if you know about the experiment, it is almost impossible to keep yourself from filling in the blank spot without hard and special training.[6]

It is easy to make one answer to all these trivial problems. We can say, "We have *learned* to do these things. We have learned the coin is round and the paper is white. The Patagonians had not learned to see large ships and doubtless would with more experience. We learned to see the world in a new way and thus understood what the Impressionist painters were saying. Soon we will learn what modern, nonrepresentational painters are saying and the world will again look different. It is all a matter of learning new things. As for filling in the blind spot in the experiment, well, doubtless, there is a similar explanation for that."

This answer is clearly true. It is the implications of it that are so startling and it is these implications we avoid. If when we learn new things we can see the world differently, then as we learn new things we react to it differently. We are then living in a different world, a world with different possibilities, different impossibilities. Which world is the right one, the real one? Is it the new world or the old? What do we mean by the question? And, ultimately the question, if this is true, what new things should we try to learn so as to live in a different world?

At least if we cannot answer these questions we have to come to agreement on one thing: We can learn to perceive the world differently, and then to act differently in this new world. This is a great step. It is not just that we must learn what is "out there" and react to it. We must learn that there is a constant interplay between our consciousness and outside "reality" wherein each affects the other.[7] Can we begin to arrive at some general idea as to how much a part our consciousness plays in this "game of give and take?"[8] How much are we responsible for? How much is already "out there" and we can only respond to it? Is our contribution a small one or a large one?

On one area of this we are clear. Whether reality is "friendly" or "unfriendly," "nice" or "not nice," "loving" or "hostile" seems to depend largely on us. We know this so well, it is said repeatedly in clichés: "When we are in love, everything is beautiful." "The pessimist sees the glass half-empty, the optimist sees it as half-full." "Beauty is in the eye of the beholder." "Keep your eye on the doughnut, not on the hole." We know that to one person the sea, or the desert or the mountains or the city, is beautiful and restful. To another person it is threatening, hostile, ugly, upsetting. One morning we arise and see the beauty in the snow. Another morning we see it as a troublesome mass of white, ugly material to be gotten through. To a lover, the loved one is beautiful. Another may strongly disagree.

One quality of reality, then, we are sure we mostly determine: its feeling-tone. We have known this so long and so well that it seems unimportant to us, but if we look at it with fresh eyes for a moment, we can begin to see how important it is. One of the great questions we started with is "What sort of universe do we live in? Is it friendly or unfriendly to man?" We now begin to understand that much of the answer to this question is our contribution to reality, that all of the answer is not "out there"; a large part of it is our own creation and maintained by us. When stated like that, this knowledge clearly has important implications for us. We will return to them later.

There is another aspect of our contribution to what is "out there" that is so commonplace and so well known that it takes a definite effort of thought to realize its importance. This is the fact that we decide what is real and important about things and what is real and unimportant. Once we have done this, our decision then makes us think and feel a certain way about the object, and any other ways of thinking and feeling about it seem silly. In other words, we decide on what is important about something, and this determines how we are able to look at it and what is really "real" about it and how we react to it. Then we feel that this is the only correct way to perceive and react to it, that we have discovered these truths, not invented them.

As an example, I list all of Rembrandt's paintings by size and tell you that compared to the Sahara Desert they are insignificant and that the paint on the largest one weighs only seven ounces. Or, a child is run over by a car and I tell you that it is not worthwhile being concerned since the total value of the chemicals that make up his body is only sixty-three dollars.[9] Or, suppose you tell me that you like a particular piece of music and plan to buy a record of it, and I reply that it has only 1863 notes in it and you would get a better bargain with another that costs the same and has 2194 notes.

In all these cases, my remarks are at best stupid, and often offensive as well. It is quite clear that I have completely missed the point in all of them. The paintings, or the child, or the music, you tell me, have quite different values and their importance lies very far from the areas of my comments. You are clearly right in this reply and in regarding my comments as those of a schizophrenic. What you are also telling me, however, is that there is a certain right way to look at things, and that these right ways are perfectly clear to anyone of reasonable soundness of mind; that things often have a clear value that seems implicit in them. This is, of course, perfectly correct, but again these are implications. The importance of things does not lie in them, although it often seems to. It is part of our contribution to reality and gives us a small clue to one part of how we do contribute to what is "out there." We begin from these more obvious examples to see that what is important about something is also largely our part of this strange game of give-and-take our consciousness plays with reality. How a thing is put together, organized, is our decision, not an implacable part of reality. And we usually interpret this value and organization as existing in the things themselves and act on this interpretation.[10]

In the sixteenth century an American Indian, according to an old story, [11] wandered into a building of the Inquisition in Spain. He saw people trying to convince others to change their statements about God, and the others refusing in the face of torture and death. The Indian was puzzled by both groups of people. Why should one group want to change the statements of another on this subject, and why should the second group refuse?

It is clear that the Indian and the Spaniards described, perceived, and reacted to reality quite differently. The members of the Inquisition and their victims saw an eternity of afterlife as an important part of reality and their present behavior as determining how they would spend it. Their viewpoint was clear: A short period of pain was as nothing compared to an eternity of bliss or torment. The Indian did not see this as a part of reality and so was completely confused by their behavior. Both the Indian and the Spaniards stood on the same portion of the earth, under the same sky, breathed the same air, and lived in quite different realities. Each culture had been taught to perceive reality in a certain way and felt that its way was the truth. If you come to the conclusion that one was right and the other wrong, you are saying that the reality one perceived is closer to the reality you have been taught to believe than is that of the other.

Three different individuals have the same repetitive dream. A deceased grandfather forces them to eat large quantities from a revolting dish. One says, "I had better stop eating heavy food in the evening." Another says, "I think I will call my psychoanalyst." The third says, "I wonder what my grandfather is trying to tell me." Each of these people clearly lives in a different world. In the first, one should stay healthy by listening to messages from the body. In the second, it is possible to get messages from the subconscious. In the third, one ought to stay in touch with ancestors. Each of these individuals has an organized and coherent world picture, an intelligible metaphysical system, although he may not have elaborated it into a psychophysiological theory of digestion, a psychoanalytical theory of dreams or a cosmology in which the living and the dead are both equally real and continue to interact.[12]

The problem is not just one of an encounter of realities in Spain in the sixteenth century. A father and son today discussing what the son should do now that he has finished high school might well face a similar situation. In the father's reality, the son should go on to college, work hard, learn a skill or profession, find a useful place in the culture he lives in, get married, amass enough worldly goods so that he can live comfortably and safely, and make a contribution to society in a way that will be both useful to others and help maintain the society that supports him. In the son's reality, he should take time to find out who he really is—what likes, dislikes, aptitudes, and style most truly reflect his own personality—and seek a life that most gardens and grows his own unique being. In this view safety, happiness, and the best life come from internal harmony and from harmony between his natural style and his behavior, rather than from outside factors such as safe and approved work, insurance policies, and the like. If you come to the conclusion that one of these two views is more correct than the other, you are stating that one is closer to your reality than the other.[13]

"Yes," one might answer, "on certain things opinions can disagree. But we can trust our senses. What we see, hear, physically feel, these we can depend on!" To this I can only reply again that there are major contributions we make to our perceptions so that here, too, we contribute a very large part of what we are so sure is out there, is "real." The next time you are driving a car in hilly country and come to a long down-slope, try turning off the motor. Wait until your car, coasting down, has picked up speed somewhere around the speed you were driving at before. Then, with the motor still turned off, press down on the gas pedal. You will experience a definite, very strong, "physical" sense of being "held back," of something wrong with the car. So real is this feeling that one psychologist who knew the experiment he was doing, insisted on having his car checked out by a mechanic.[14]

Take two ordinary spoons. Place one in the freezing compartment of your refrigerator. Hold the other in your closed fist. When one is icy cold and the other reaches body temperature, fit them together and touch your arm with the tips of the two spoons at the same time. Here is a "cold" object and a "warm" object very close to each other, touching you simultaneously. Your skin will report to you that you are being touched by one "hot" object. "Cold" and "warm" have, with the aid of the contribution you make to "reality," added up to "hot."

Or, read the captions and look at the same picture of men on a picket line in two newspapers of opposite political persuasions. In one paper you will see bigoted, selfish, angry men. In the other you will see, with equal clarity, idealistic and determined men.

Look out the window of a railway train and watch the train moving past outside objects. Focus your vision on a point on the glass and watch the objects outside suddenly start to slide backward.

A series of still photographs is flashed on a screen. There is no movement on the screen, only the succession of slightly different pictures. You, however, see movement as clearly as if you were watching a person walk across the room.

Watch one of those flashing electric signs in which by turning off one pattern of lights just before another is turned on, the first set is made to seem to move across the distance to the second set. It looks like the figure of a man in the lights is actually moving his legs while the "truth" is that two separate sets of lights outlining legs are alternately flashing on and off. The movement is a clear and strong perception, as clear as *anything else you see*. There is, however, no movement; that is your contribution. Can you tell the difference between what you discover out there and what you invent? What criteria do you use to say that one perception can be trusted to tell you the truth of what is real and another cannot be trusted?

It would be easy to go on giving examples of this sort. We could start with the football quarterback who gets a "green-stick" fracture of his leg in the first play of a quarter and does not notice it until the end of the quarter when it doubles him up in anguish, and ask when the pain started to be "real." We could end with the stars in the Big Dipper or the Southern Cross that appear so *obviously* to be a part of a pattern, but that, from an astronomer's viewpoint, have absolutely nothing to do with each other. But our reply to the statement that the senses can be trusted and will tell us what is "real" is clear. We organize reality even as we think we see or hear or touch what is out there. Alas, it begins to appear that we may never be able to know exactly what is out there, but can only be aware of, know about, a combination, an alloy of reality and ourselves.[15]

"All this is very fine," we say, "but twist and turn as you will, chop logic and move words around all you want, the world is still made up of real things, things we can touch, see, hear, taste, smell. They are what count. All the rest is words."

It is clear that this argument feels right. It seems so true that everything else seems meaningless. Let us look at it a little further.

A pianist sits down at his piano and begins to press keys down with his fingers. The keys move small hammers that, striking tensed wires, produce notes. These notes are individual sounds, vibrations in the air, coming one after the other. They are real things, these packets of vibrations, that fit our definition. Presently we realize we are enjoying the melody. Then we ask, "Where did the melody come from?" The pianist is still only pressing the keys, the hammers are still only making the notes. The melody is clearly not in these. The pianist could strike entirely different notes by playing in a different key and we would still hear the same melody. Where did it come from? Is it a solid *thing* we can point to? Is it real? It is certainly—if we like music—the most important thing going on. But where did it come from? The notes would be there even if we were not in the room; the vibrations of the notes would be moving through the air. Would the melody also be there? It seems clear that for the melody to exist our contribution is needed. We are a part of its creation. It is not in the air vibrations we call the notes that are in the room with or without a listener. The melody is different. It is only there if someone listens to the notes, and contributes to its coming into existence. And yet, it clearly seems to us the most important and real thing going on when the pianist is at work. Are we coming here to the conclusion that what we help create tends to be the most important aspects of reality? If true, this could be very important.

Not only do I organize the way I perceive—react to the "things" in the world—I also do the same with myself and with my relationships with other people. If I am one of four people sitting at a bridge table I may be responding to a group of four, to four separate individuals, or to any other combination. However, as soon as we start to play bridge I perceive two pairs of people and behave appropriately. This perception of the two pairs of people is as strong and seems as "objective" as did my perception of the melody.[16]

What we are finding out is that the usual view of reality and how we learn about it, has it, at least partly, backward. This usual view is that we first observe the universe and, on the basis of our observations, make a definition, a description of it. The truth seems much closer—at least half the distance closer—to the other view: that our culture and home provide us with a way of describing reality, and when we look at the universe, that is what we see. We have, so to speak, the map first and when we look, Lo! we see reality following the map. Although there is a strong tendency in us to decide that one of these two views is the correct one, long centuries of philosophic study have taught us that the truth lies somewhere between them.

It is true, however, that "common sense" tells us that we make the map, the description of reality, on the basis of what we observe. When we look closely, though, we see that we observe only what we are prepared in advance to see. One philosopher described the "common-sense" view as similar to the comment of the artillery sergeant who said that cannons were made by taking a hole and enclosing it in steel. He had it backward, but somehow it sounded reasonable.[17] The poet-philosopher, Goethe, summed up the opposite view when he wrote, "Whatever is fact was first in theory."

Physicists and Firewalking:
How Much Can
Realities Differ?

II

As we look at all this, an answer to one of our questions begins to form. We asked, "Is it possible to get some clues as to how much of the reality we live in we invent and how much we discover?" Or, to put it in other words, "What and how large is our contribution to reality?" Now we begin to see certain things about the answer to these questions. Our contribution includes the decision as to what the important aspects of a situation are; what should be considered important and what should be considered unimportant about it. Our contribution also includes its feeling-tone, whether it is regarded as good or bad, pleasant or unpleasant, attractive or unattractive. It also includes deciding on what level it should be reacted to: as notes, for example, or as melody. Also, its relation to anything else, including ourselves, is largely contributed by us.

Are these contributions important parts of reality? Certainly they are the parts that shape our reactions to a thing, that determine our behavior. They seem to be aspects of what we generally would consider the most important parts of reality, those parts that most strongly affect our behavior. This is a curious and startling finding and not one we would have expected as we began our search.

The obvious comment to all this is clear: "You talk of changing realities as if you were talking of the possibility of some major change. Yet, everything said so far is about changing attitudes or learning more about a situation so that we can see into it more deeply and react to it more appropriately. The rules, the laws, of all the realities you describe so far are pretty much—if not exactly—the same. If this is all you mean by different realities, it is really all pretty small stuff."

To answer this, let me describe the structure of a reality that anyone of reasonably good intelligence can learn with a fair amount of hard work (I never promised you it would be easy) to operate in and to accomplish major events in, events he or she could not possibly accomplish while operating in the ordinary reality.

In this particular reality, there is no such thing as a separate object; all things and events flow into each other so that it is impossible to say where one leaves off and the other begins. It is often not possible to say that two events occurred in the same place or same time or, frequently, to say which one occurred first and which second. Further, cause and effect often do not operate in making things happen and "good" and "bad" are not meaningful words or concepts in this reality.

Clearly, this is a quite different reality from the one we ordinarily operate in. It is, however, exactly as real as our usual one and can be used quite as effectively for some purposes, although it is pretty nearly useless for some other purposes. It is the reality used by a relativity physicist when he is going about his daily work, and there is little question in most of our minds how effective the work of relativity physicists can be.

This is one of the realities that human beings can achieve, and certainly the rules of it are far different from our usual ones. As we shall see, we can learn to perceive— react to the world in a number of startlingly different ways, and to change the reality we live in to a very great degree. It is true that I have been starting with small examples, minor modifications of our reality, but this is so that we can gradually become accustomed to the idea, learn to work with it and to keep a confident and easy control while we decide on the changes we wish to make, and work to accomplish these changes.

(In addition, I have avoided here, and will continue to avoid, the use of long references to and quotations from the philosophers who have spent so much serious time and effort exploring the nature of "reality" and of the "human-reality" interaction. These are generally written in a specialized language that, without training in it, can make for some pretty hard slogging. For those, however, who would wish to have the formal philosophical position I am using clearly stated in this way, I have included reference no. *18* in the notes.)

A group of individuals carefully prepare themselves psychologically. For a longer or shorter period they chant, pray, meditate, or do whatever their particular culture tells them is the right technique of preparation. Then they dig a long, shallow trench in the ground and burn wood in it until it is filled with white-hot coals. They remove their sandals or shoes and slowly walk barefoot the length of the trench. At the end of the trench they step out upon solid ground with unburned feet. If they were wearing clothes, these are not scorched, although a cloth held a few feet from the side of the trench will scorch and burn.

Whether you like or accept the idea or not, this procedure is followed fairly routinely in a dozen or so cultures. No one who has studied this phenomenon ever seriously suggested that it was faked. Anthropologists and curious visitors have closely watched the process from beginning to end. The only way you can deny its existence is to claim it is impossible and that it therefore never happened, and that it is therefore obvious that everyone who reported it was lying or was somehow fooled. Of course, you can't say it is impossible without saying that you know everything important about reality and that your knowledge is so complete it can have no surprises for you, but you don't have to think about that if you don't want to.[19] It is easier to say it is obvious it never happened and to forget the entire thing. Then you can relax comfortably in your culture's definition of what reality "really is" and not be bothered. This lessens your responsibility for your own life considerably.

Nevertheless it does happen[20] and it is impossible by our

cultural—and therefore by our personal—definition of reality. The only possible way out of this that I can see is that there are other, equally valid, definitions of reality, and in one of these this procedure of "firewalking" is possible. The careful psychological preparation by the participants thus becomes a procedure for changing their definition of reality. It is clear that not only do other definitions exist, but that these others include some that are very different from our ordinary definition. A parapsychologist sits in his laboratory before a curious apparatus. There is a wide table with a line down the center of its length. Above the end of the table is a cup with a hinged bottom leading to a long trough down to the table and ending exactly on the midline. Hanging from the ceiling is a camera. The parapsychologist looks at a record counter next to the table to see what number it is up to. It is 35,073, which is an odd number, so he concentrates on "left." (If it had been an even number he would have concentrated on "right.") He then presses a button and an electromagnetic relay opens the hinged door of the cup, a dozen dice rattle down the trough to scatter across the table, and the camera clicks, photographing where they have stopped. The counter goes to the next number. The parapsychologist picks up the dice and drops them back in the cup. He then repeats the entire procedure until he has done it, over a period of months, a hundred thousand times.[21]

When the analysis is made from the photographs it shows that the dice had a slight, but real ("statistically significant") tendency to end up to the left of the table's center line more often on odd numbers and to the right more often on even numbers. (Technically we call this "psychokinesis" and I will discuss a more dramatic example of it later when I describe a fascinating phenomenon known as "Phillip.")

Now, this is clearly impossible. It is a primary law of our ordinary way of constructing reality that "Mind" cannot affect "Matter" directly.[22] Nevertheless, there it is, and under careful laboratory conditions, repeated by other parapsychologists in *their* laboratories. You have a limited number of choices as to what you can do with this data. You can ignore it, you can say the statistical method is invalid. Or, you can come to the conclusion, that since it cannot happen in the usual way we invent–discover reality and yet it does happen, there must be another way of inventing–discovering reality that is so *different* from our usual way that in it "Mind" *can* affect "Matter" directly. I do not know of any other useful choices.

As to the first choice of ignoring the data, be my guest if that's what you want to do, but you don't solve many problems that way. If you choose the second choice of denying the validity of the statistical method, you must— if you want to be honest with yourself—also then throw out all those other sciences that largely depend on it. This includes quanta mechanics, sociology, geology, much of astronomy, and a number of others. If you do not choose one of the first two choices, this seems to leave you with the third.

There are other kinds of facts that suggest to us that there is more to "what is" than would fit into the ordinary, everyday way we invent–discover reality. I shall be discussing some of these at various points in this book. There is one set of facts, however, that also suggests that in some way we already know this and sometimes react to special situations in terms of it. These facts consist of what the sociologist Peter Berger has called signals of transcendence. By this term he means certain human behavior patterns, found in every culture we know of, that simply and clearly imply a completely different kind of reality from our ordinary one. We *behave* as if we know more exists than our usual reality and it is our behavior rather than our words that most clearly reveals our beliefs, our orientations, and our knowledge.

Berger describes five kinds of signals of transcendence although, as he says, there are certainly more. I would like to describe three of these: the appeal to order, the appeal to play, and the appeal to damnation. I shall only discuss these very briefly and not give the detail presented in Berger's lively and important book, *A Rumor of Angels*. My goal here is simply to point out that these three classes of behavior all indicate our deep beliefs that we are also at home in the universe in quite different ways from the one we would ordinarily describe.

The appeal to order is best illustrated by the behavior of a mother when a child is frightened at night and wakes in darkness and chaos with no firm foundation to depend on. She comforts the child by saying, in effect, "Everything is all right. Everything is in order. Don't be afraid." She is in effect saying, "Have trust in being in the world." The important aspect of this in our context is that if all reality is summed up in our everyday view of it, the mother is lying. What she would be asking the child to have trust in, and not be frightened by, is a world that will eventually kill both mother and child and annihilate them both. Whether or not she *should* lie and comfort the child, if this is what she truly believes, is not relevant here. The relevant fact is that if she believed only in her everyday world, she would be lying when she comforted the child—and she is not lying. She is showing her own belief in more than her senses reveal by honestly comforting the child. This is a signal of transcendence, "a sign of our knowledge of another than our everyday way of being in reality; ...a way in which love is not annihilated by death and in which, therefore, the trust in the power of love to banish chaos is justified."[23]

A second set of signals of transcendence is in play where we move out of our usual laws and truths about reality and feel free to shift time, place, and person as we wish. We set up a special way of ordering the world and its rules are far from the everyday ones. In all human cultures we do this and the rules we set up are identical. We act as if these rules are valid for our purposes and get much enjoyment and benefit thereby. As we play in the shadow of our approaching death we act as if our mortality, our usual conceptions of time and space and causality are not, for the moment, valid. This, too, is a signal of transcendence.

A third set of signals is called by Berger the appeal to damnation. Certain acts arouse in us such a fundamental sense of outrage, wrongness, and injustice that we do not believe any repayment on earth as we know it would be sufficient. Literally, these acts cry out to heaven and we have the sense that even killing the person responsible would not be enough. What *does* one do with an Eichmann? Or, with the people at Ravensbruck Concentration Camp who had a special barracks for pregnant women where there was extra food so that their strength would be kept up, and who, when the labor pains started, chained the woman's ankles together and left her in the middle of the barracks square until she died? Or, the guards at Dachau who forced parents to watch the brutal murder of all their children under seven years of age, and at the same time played lullabies on the camp loudspeaker system? We feel that there exists somewhere a justice that will adequately answer these acts, but that no punishment on earth would be enough, that even slow torture to death for these guards would be insufficient. And in this feeling we reveal a belief that there is more to reality than we ordinarily conceive, for only in a world of larger or different dimensions than our senses show could there exist the punishment we would feel adequate.

Berger discusses other sets of signals of transcendence such as hope and humor. These are all basic and universal human activities that reveal our belief in something other than the world of our senses.

There is an old Zen story about the two monks who were arguing about a flag waving in the wind. One said, "It is the flag that is waving." The other disagreed and said, "It is the wind that is waving." They went to the abbot of the monastery about the problem. He said both were wrong. "It is the mind that is waving."

As we read this, it sounds like a typical Zen story with its paradoxes and its use of different levels of language to attempt to loosen our over-firm belief that we know what reality is. We can find, however, an example or two that are more convincing. Let us look at the following drawings for a moment.

As we look at the cube, it shifts on us. First we are looking at it from one perspective, then from another. As far as we can tell, we are not "doing" anything. The cube

RUBIN FACE VASE

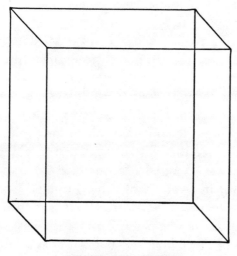

NECKER CUBE

itself appears to shift. It seems to us as if reality itself is changing under our eyes. This is the clear feeling we have before we dismiss the entire problem by deciding it is simply an "optical illusion." Similarly, when we look at the Rubin Figure it seems to shift by itself from a vase to two faces and back again.

Of course, these are optical illusions. The implications, however, are more important than that. When we examine our perception and feeling, we find that it seems to us that the cube is moving. Then we decide that it "really" is the mind that is moving. Perhaps there was more to the Zen story than we first realized.

Several points are critical here. First, our clear feeling that the changes lie in outside reality and our later understanding that this is not so. Surely this is a simple example, but we shall have to find out how far this simple example is repeated in more complex ways in other, more important, aspects of the relations between "ourselves" and "reality."

A second critical point is also implied here. The perceptions we have are not entirely up to us. Try as we will, we cannot make the cube appear to be an ice cream cone. Whatever is "out there" plays a part in our perception and response. The way we perceive the outside world is determined by a combination of "us" and "it"; no explanation that it is either all one or all the other will stand up very long. I can perceive Beethoven's Ninth Symphony in a variety of ways. I can listen to the music and be one with it. I can react to it as individual notes. I can analyze the themes. I can perceive–react to it as a historical or sociological document or as a design in black and white. I cannot, however, perceive it as "God Save the Queen" or as an automobile.

There *are* limits to the part I can play in determining the reality I live in. The point of this book is that we are much less limited than we have hitherto supposed, and that this fact offers us vast opportunities for the enrichment and development of our lives. The limits do exist, however. If, to paraphrase an example of Bertrand Russell, I line up three people, Tom, Dick and Josephine, a hundred yards apart in a straight line, and then a quarter-mile in front of Tom I shoot off a concealed cannon, certain predictable things will happen. First, Tom will hear the sound, then after a definite interval Dick will hear it, and after an equal interval Josephine will hear it. Clearly, *something* passed over the space at a definite speed. It is extremely unlikely that I can arrange the order my three friends hear the sound so that, staying in the same positions, Dick hears it first, then Josephine, then Tom. Reality is only partly our invention; it is also partly our discovery. Our task is to discover how much and in what areas which is which; and then to determine how much new freedom this gives us and what we can do with it.

Incomplete Maps and
Human Freedom
III

Our discussion so far leads us now to the concept of the map. A world-picture, a system of describing how the world works, is a map of reality. As with any map, certain definitions of what "exists" and is "real" are accepted, others are rejected. A map says, "What I show is real for your purpose, what I do not show is not real for your purpose." It defines reality and its definition is valid so long as your goals are those that can be accomplished best with this definition. Let us take an example.

In the next two pages let us imagine two maps of the area around New York City. One map is the one a pilot of a private plane might use on a clear day. He looks down from his airplane and sees rivers, bridges, buildings, etc., knows from them where he is and how to get to the airport. The other map is the one the pilot of a commercial airliner will generally use. It shows radio beacons only. These are two maps of what is "out there" in the same geographical space, both accurate and valid, both useful, and do not have a single feature in common. We could make the point further by imagining other kinds of maps of the same area such as barometric maps, population density maps, soil sample maps, or what-have-you. Each would show a different picture, contain different entities, lead to different behavior, and be useful for accomplishing different goals. Each would be *a* valid map, none *the* valid map.[24]

This last point is one of the major differences between a physical map and a world-picture. When we look at a map, we know it is only valid for some purposes and not for others. It does not contain the premise that it is the *only* right way of looking at the territory. A world-picture almost invariably contains this false premise, and this tends to get us humans into much of the trouble we are in. We forget it can, as a physical map can, only help us to accomplish certain goals. The others it defines as non-existent or unreal and thereby leads those parts of our being that would be nourished by those goals to wither unfulfilled.

So firmly are we inwardly convinced that the system of organizing reality we are using is the only valid and "real" one that it is even very difficult for us to comprehend the idea that the symbols our system uses are not an inextricable part of what they represent. In other words, it feels to us as if the symbols our culture has taught us to use are the naturally right ones and that any other symbol would be wrong. If you pronounce the word "igle" to two people, an American and a German, it sounds to the American as if no other thing than a bird could have this name, and to the German as if no other thing than a hedgehog could have it.[25] Or, look at the statement, "2 + 2 = 4." It is hard to believe that the "+" sign could equally well stand for "divided by." We are so well trained that the concept "plus" seems the only possible natural and right one for the sign "+". The designation originally was quite accidental and could have been "divided by" just as easily, but it's pretty hard to get yourself to really believe this.

There is an old story that illustrates our feelings here. Adam and Eve were naming animals in the Garden of Eden. Eve looked at one and said, "That's a hippopotamus." Adam asked why she gave it that name and Eve replied, "Because it *looks* like a hippopotamus." And to us today, indeed it does. It would be pretty difficult for any of us to rename a hippopotamus a "phlerm" without the secret reservation of saying to yourself, "I'm calling it a phlerm but it's *really* a hippopotamus." The symbols and the map of reality we are trained in both seem to us to be the only possible valid ones.

One thing should be clear about your reality, the world you operate in, that you perceive and react to: It is capable of change. In order to begin to look at this possibility, I am going to discuss some aspects of realities starting with the number of ideas in them and their scope.

In the fifteenth century, the world's greatest engineer designed a helicopter. Leonardo da Vinci's flying machine is perfectly airworthy and would fly except for one thing. In his perception of reality, there was no trace of an idea that every eight-year-old child has today. This idea is that power may be obtained from things other than wind, water, or muscle. This was simply not in his reality. As a result, when the problem arose of how to make the propellers turn, all he could do was station two men in the helicopter, turning cranks. This did not provide enough power compared to the weight of the two men so it could not fly. From what we know about Leonardo's ability, it seems pretty clear that if he had had the idea of a non-wind, water, or muscle source, he would have pretty quickly produced a working steam engine and, for better or worse, the helicopter would have been flying five centuries before it did.

This sounds like a mildly interesting historical fact. It has, however, implications today. The incident discussed earlier of the father and son discussing the son's life plans may be a case in point. The son's idea that the greatest good for the individual and for society comes from each individual learning wholeheartedly to sing his own unique song, to beat out his individual music in ways of being, relating, creating, may not be an idea that exists in the father's reality. It is a crucial idea in the son's. Conversely, the idea that anything of value in life takes hard work and interior discipline may be in the father's reality and not in the son's. Unless each can learn to listen to the other, to perceive each other's reality, they may sit in the same room, look at each other from a three-foot distance, and talk at each other, but there will be little communication and neither will change or grow through the experience any more than did the Indian and the Spaniards in our other example. Literally, neither is free, has free will, as both are bound to respond appropriately to their realities, and since they do not conceive of another "real" reality, have no options to change their behavior.

Up to the present few years, the whole problem of ecology—literally, the problem of not turning our only planet into an uninhabitable garbage dump—has been an impossible one, because two of the ideas needed to make positive ecological changes were not in the realities of most people. These two ideas, that everything is connected to everything else and that everything has to go somewhere, were as far away from most people's perceived-reacted to worlds as was the idea of the gasoline engine from Leonardo's. It is only, however, as these two ideas become a part of people's realities that ecology can become a meaningful activity.

Our realities do change with time as new ideas become a part of them. That human beings have an unconscious mind, that the world is round, that we can communicate at a distance immediately, that bacteria exist, that emotions can affect the body, are only a few of the new ideas that have become part of our realities. Since new ideas can be accepted by us and can change the world we live in, each of us can ask ourselves what new ideas (like the power source of Leonardo) we need to solve those problems that are important for us now. We can keep open an eye that looks for the new idea and check and test it. We can introduce as our first new idea the idea that our ideas (and therefore the world we live in) can change, be added to, become richer. And by this concept we have already introduced a major change in our reality; we have made it open to new changes if they are the sort we need.

Another aspect of a person's reality that can change is its scope: How much does it include? We can look at one aspect of this by asking the question: "How many people are in it?" By this I mean to ask how many people are so real to you that you act as if they were as real as you are? Are there any besides yourself? One, two, or three, or so? Family? Friends? The people you work with? Is a starving child in another country real enough to you so that when you vote or when you decide how you feel about taxes or rationing or a charity drive, you take the child into serious account? Different people have different numbers of others in their realities.

Historically, the scope of their reality has changed for most people by growing larger. If we view the problem in terms of the willingness to act, perhaps to defend, fight for, and even die for, we can see this clearly. First it was probably only the self or self plus immediate family. Then it increased to the tribe, the city, the province, and the nation.

Each increase in the scope of a reality included all those within it rather than replacing them. And interestingly enough, our feelings are quite different about people who have a wider reality than we do, than they are about people who have a narrower reality than ours. Think how you would feel about someone who would only fight for a province rather than a nation. Let us say he or she would defend Burgundy or New Jersey instead of France or the United States. Then think how you would feel about someone who regards the entire planet as his reality, a Dag Hammarskjöld or an Albert Schweitzer. Quite obviously, these are different feelings.

Once you are aware of this, of the scope of your reality,

you can make a decision how you feel about it; whether or not you wish to change it. This is the first step and a crucial one: To be aware of an aspect of your reality, to know that it can be changed and to decide whether or not you wish to change it.

Are there examples in which our contribution to what is out there have changed, and therefore our perception of the world and our behavior has followed suit? Certainly this has been repeatedly true of our judgments of what is beautiful. There have been considerable periods of time in which Michelangelo was considered a second-rate sculptor, and periods in which Shakespeare was considered a minor Elizabethan playwright. Examples of this sort could be multiplied endlessly. We might, also, however, look at our views on children. It is only quite recently that they changed to the degree that we stopped seven- and eight-year-old children from being taken out of school and sent to work for ten to twelve hours a day in factories. At the time we were passing these laws, only fifty to sixty years ago, was there a change out there in the children that made us change our behavior toward them? Clearly not; it was a change in our contribution to reality; to what was out there. It is even possible that we will again change our contribution as to what is real and what is important in reality and come to the conclusion that the price of your car is less important than your children's health. If we did that, we would change our behavior by passing real anti-pollution laws.

There is no such thing as *the* size of space. "How large is space?" is not a meaningful question. "How large is space for me?" is. We can legitimately ask, and reasonably expect to get an answer to, this second question. The size of space in your reality is just large enough to contain and separate all the objects and people you react to as if they were really real and existing now. These people and objects must affect your behavior, as this is the working definition of "real" to you.[26]

Just as your space is just large enough to contain and separate all entities you react to as existing now, "time" is similarly defined. We cannot ask, and hope for a meaningful answer to, the question, "How long is time?" We can ask, "How long is time for me?" Time, for you, is just long-enough to contain and separate all entities and actions that you react to as if they were real. If you react to problems that may arise in twenty years, as by saving for retirement, your time is at least twenty years long into the future. If you react now to incidents and atmospheres of your childhood, as we have learned that we all do to a greater or lesser degree, your real time stretches at least that far into the past. A historian who perceives present events that affect him and his behavior as being a part of a sequence of events that occurred before he was born has a real time that stretches even further into the past. If you react to what may happen after your biological death, as in working to prevent future population or ecological disasters, then your time is "real" at least that far into the future.

Perhaps this will become somewhat clearer if we reflect that we would not, today, ask, "How many numbers are there?" but rather "How many numbers are real to you?" At the extremes we can contrast the primitive, who can count to ten but who calls the next number "many," and the mathematician. But I can also estimate my own limits. Up to a certain point, I react differently to each number. After that limit, only to larger differences (as between 100 and 125, but not between 100 and 101). And there is a limit where further additions simply do not make a difference in my behavior. I do not think, for example, that I would behave differently toward a million (anything) and two million of the same entities. A "millionaire," a statistician for the Census Bureau, or a comptroller of a large company would feel quite otherwise.

There is a further aspect to your perception of both time and space. Does your reality have these as composed of sharp areas limited by boundaries (as the surface of a checkerboard might be seen) or as a "seamless garment"? Do you perceive–react to your time as composed of definitely limited periods or as the flow of a river, of which no part can be marked off as really separate from the others? Is space a series of concentric circles around you (or, my family, my friends, my town, my country, etc.) so that you behave differently toward events between each pair of circling lines? Or, do you perceive–react to your space as having no limitations within it so that all events and entities are inextricably interwoven to the extent that, as the physicist P. C. Bridgeman put it, "any local agitation shakes the entire universe"? As we shall see when we discuss different world-pictures, this is an important aspect of your reality and one subject to your decision to change it.

I wrote earlier of the problem of Voltaire's story of the Indian who wandered into the Inquisition and was confused by the actions of the people involved. It is clear that the Indian and the Spaniards were organizing reality in different ways and were, therefore, perceiving–reacting to quite different pictures of reality. This is something we human beings are capable of: of organizing reality in different ways and thereby changing it. It is extremely unlikely that animals have this ability to anything like the degree that we have. An animal seems to be very limited in its choices.

It is true that animals also use several descriptions of reality. A strong drive—protection, hunger, sex—coming into dominance in the animal will restructure the universe and give objects different meanings. The hermit crab will perceive-react to an anemone as food, a shelter, or a device, depending on which is his strongest drive at the moment.[27] There is no communication between the different organizations of reality; they are "as separate as the different scenes on a revolving stage."[28]

The difference between humans and animals here is that not only do human beings have a potentially very much wider range of choices, they can also exercise their special human prerogative and *choose* which organization of reality will be most effective to attain their goals. The animal automatically shifts as its drives shift. Human beings can do otherwise.

A definition of "human being" begins to emerge here. A human being is an organizer of reality with a wide variety of options. The more he exercises these options, the more human and the less animal he or she is. Being human is here defined in the manner of modern science, not by what something—here a person—*is*, but by what he or she *does*. The science of the Renaissance defined things primarily in terms of structure (what are its component parts?); science today defines things primarily in terms of process (what does it do?). In terms of the wide variety of human options, perhaps then we can define a human being in terms of having and exercising this choice of options and say that the more it is exercised, the more the special human function is being exercised.

The reverse of our definition of human being is also true. The less a person exercises this option, the less he is aware of different, valid possibilities of organizing reality, of perceiving–reacting to it, the less he is using of his specially human potential. He may be brilliant and able in dealing with the particular organization of reality he considers the only "real" one, but he is bound to respond to anything that happens in an appropriate manner (appropriate to the only way he can perceive the world); and therefore he is limited and his free will is lessened.

This concept leads to another: *No one world-picture works completely.* It is not a map of reality, it is a map of one way of organizing reality. It rests on taking certain basic things on faith (in mathematics we call these axioms and know that they can never be proven), and on excluding certain things as not being a part of the system; of being "unreal."[29] Because of these factors, all metaphysical systems, all world-pictures, "limp"; they work well for some purposes, poorly for others. None encompasses *all* human needs. Those, for example, that deal effectively with questions of "how to" deal less effectively (or not at all) with questions of "why" and vice versa. Those that satisfy our needs for predicting and controlling reality do not satisfy our needs for meaning. The converse is also true.

It appears that it is partly for this reason that human beings have always been ineffective in dealing with their total life problems. We have always been unbalanced in one area or another. (There have probably been a few individual exceptions to this, but they are rare indeed.) Nowhere in human history that we know of have we been able to live what is clearly our potential in joy, zest, productiveness, love, kindness. It is clear that we have a high potential in all of these, since we have seen ourselves and others living closer to this potential in one or the other of them at various periods of our life. Also, we recognize our respect for and admiration of those who live closer to this potential in one of them, and our even greater respect for those who live it in more than one.

It seems, then, as if our crippled behavior toward ourselves, others, and our planet may well be due in part to the fact that we live in a perceived–reacted to universe that is incomplete by its very nature. We are held in this invented–discovered reality by the fact that it is a premise of every world-picture that it is the *only* picture of truth, a premise that it is not possible to be "realistic" and accept—or even seriously consider—any other. And, being forced to live in a universe that can fill only part of our human needs, we thrash about in agony attacking first ourselves, then our neighbor, and have little real concern for the general nature that sustains us.

The answer, if this concept has validity, is to increase the number of world-pictures we can perceive–react to, so that we may fulfill *all* of our human needs. We may then *choose* which conception of reality fits the needs we have predominant at the moment. We cannot do this, of course, until we are clear that none of the valid systems of organizing reality is closer to *truth* than the others; that each is a different way of perceiving and reacting to what *is*.

A new definition of "freedom" begins to appear from

our search. Freedom begins to look like the ability to search for new forms of relationship between our "self" and what is "out there." To the degree we can look for new ways to conceive of, to describe, reality, we are free; to the degree we cannot make this search, we are not free but bound to react "appropriately" to the reality our culture has given us. We must, so long as this for us is the only conceivable reality, respond appropriately to it. And in this "appropriate" set of responses, we are not free. When, however, we have other tools, other ways of creating reality, other ways of organizing and relating the "self" and what is "out there," we are free to choose among the different ways, each with a different set of appropriate responses, and we become more free.

Psychology, Philosophy, and Modes of Being
IV

Our cultural division of reality into what is "out there" and what is "in here" is known to all of us quite clearly. Out there, things are real, permanent, and common to all who are not either insane or maimed in a sense receptor system. In here, things are imaginary, rather transient, and private. This system of dividing up the universe has proven very useful for advances in knowledge in certain areas, in studying what we defined as out there; but has resulted in a heavy liability in our attempts to understand what was in here. It has also made hopeless any attempt to answer what I have earlier called the big questions.[30]

It is gradually becoming clear that modern psychology has made very little progress. The advances in physics and chemistry have been very large; by comparison, those in the human sciences, which attempted to use the same methods that were so useful to the physical sciences, have been quite small. One reason for this is now becoming apparent. The physical sciences based their work on this separation of what was "inside" and what was "outside" of the human being's mind. There was, they said, the physical world of things and the mental world of ideas and feelings. This separation proved tremendously useful (up to a certain point, now passed) in physics and the other sciences of the same sort. It was simply not useful to those sciences concerned with the mental, emotional life of man or with his behavior. Psychology, however, in its attempt to prove itself a *real* science, and using this system of dividing up reality, took as its model the assumption of last century's physics that reality could be so divided into a mental and a physical world, and that these two, although they affected each other, were quite separate. Using such an assumption that did not fit its needs, psychology could only move slowly indeed.

So impressive were these developments in prediction and control of nineteenth-century physics and chemistry that it was only natural for scientists to try to proceed on the same basis to study human behavior. Here the tool failed almost completely, as it was not designed for, nor adapted to, the questions and problems. In line with our human tendency to try even harder when a technique or theory or philosophy does not work—if the nut will not fit on the bolt, we tend to try to hammer it, force it somehow—the philosophy of the nineteenth-century physical sciences was pushed to its logical extreme. Since this science considered only what was out there as real and what was in here as unreal, then the next step is that there is nothing in here; that the mental and emotional should be treated as if they do not exist. A movement in psychology led by John B. Watson, with this viewpoint, developed in the early twentieth century. This psychology acted as if only behavior could be regarded as real and as if thoughts and feelings were nonexistent. It is one of the clearest examples of how any world-picture operates. What it is not designed to study does not exist; the questions it cannot answer are not valid questions. The psychology designed by Watson and his followers, built on the model of nineteenth-century physics, came so completely to the view that thought and mind were nonexistent that they decided that when people believed they were thinking, they were just having an "illusion" caused by small rapid movements of their voice box; they were really talking silently, not thinking. At one point, there was a debate on this subject between the historian Will Durant and John B. Watson. After the debate went on for a while, Durant turned to the audience and said, "There is no point in going on with this discussion. It is clear that this is a subject about which Dr. Watson has already made up his larynx!"

The modern development of this point of view is in the work of a psychologist named B. F. Skinner and his students. This has even developed into a psychotherapy method that treats the patient as an object, something out there, and trains him to regard himself in the same way, as something to be manipulated in the same way a nineteenth-century physicist would manipulate an electric battery, some wires, and a buzzer. From my own viewpoint, this is a classic example of using a metaphysical system to try to solve problems and to answer questions for which it was not designed and for which it is irrelevant.

The way a language works makes it particularly difficult to understand that reality is a combination of what is out there plus our contribution, our organizing of it. A language, any language, is built on a particular idea of how everything is put together, and every time we use it makes us feel that its particular idea is right and all others are crazy. In fact, it is terribly hard to even think about any other view of how things are in a language built on a specific viewpoint.

In our language we are constantly told that all things out there are real and continue to be just what they are, no matter if we are present or not, or if we are thinking about them or not. Look at how it works. "The grass is green," "the wood is hard," "the car has four doors." What do these sentences tell us? They tell us that things (grass, wood, cars) are out there and have qualities (green, hard, doors) and that that is what is real. We are constantly trained to think in this way by our language and find it very hard to think in any other way. Any sentence is a picture of a state of affairs and this state of affairs includes a description of how things basically are.[31] The sentences in our language all include the idea that things are out there, separate from us in here, and have qualities that go on without any help from us. Every time we use a sentence, we are trained a bit more in believing that this is true and that any other way of describing or understanding reality is an insane one.

This is true of all languages, not just our own. One of

the things that students of language have been finding out is that a language has two purposes. To communicate, surely, is one of them. The other, equally important, is to make sure that all members of a culture have basically the same experience, that they construe reality in the same way.[32]

This, of course, is why our language is so unsuccessful in describing many things. For the description of feelings, deep emotional experiences—love, for example—it is indeed inadequate. This is because our language is designed, on the basis of our world-view, to describe and communicate and analyze only what is considered real, what is out there. Emotional experiences are not out there and so the language can only describe them by comparing them with things we consider to be "objective," physically real. We feel hot with rage, cold with anger, blue with depression, sharp with curiosity, low with depression, high with elation, glowing with love. These analyses do communicate somewhat, but for more complete expression of the inexpressible in our language we need other types of language; we need languages not split by the in-here, out-there concept. Thus, we use music and poetry. The difference between music and verbal language is easily clear, the difference between poetry and verbal language is less clear to many. Poetry is not *just* a pleasant rearrangement of words with the correct meter and rhyme. When it is, it is a jingle, a rhyme, but not poetry. As an example, I might suggest that the most perfect arrangement of words—insofar as meter and rhyme go—in the English language is an advertisement found in the window of many stores, which is clearly not poetry. It is:

Cold Beer
Sold Here.

Poetry is far more than this, it is a different *kind* of language, a language built on a different world-picture and with assets and liabilities different from those of verbal language. You do not use poetry to give directions on how to change spark plugs; it is not designed for, nor adequate for this. You do use it to describe and communicate feelings and emotions for which verbal language is not designed or adequate.

We can see how far poetry is from the technically perfect beer advertisement when e. e. cummings writes:

"Such was a poet, and shall be and is,
Who'll solve the depths of horror to defend
A sunbeam's architecture with his life,
And carve immortal jungles of despair
To hold a mountain's heartbeat in his hand."

Or, Nikos Kazantzakis says:

"I said to the almond tree,
'Sister, speak to me of God,'
And the almond tree blossomed."

Or, when A. E. Housman describes the situation at Thermopylae where the largest army the world had ever known marched against three hundred Spartan soldiers sworn to stop them or die:

"The King with half the East at heel has marched
    from lands of morning,
His fighters drink the rivers up, their shafts
    benight the air.

And he that stands shall die for nought and home
there's no returning.
The Spartans on the sea-wet rock sat down and
combed their hair."

The term "reality," or "description of reality," has the
disadvantage of sounding as if we were talking about what
is out there. This is how we are used to defining this term.
For this reason I am going to introduce a synonym for it,
"mode of being," and use the two interchangeably. Mode
of being implies we are talking about what is in here;
reality implies the opposite. Using the two interchangeably can help us become more aware that we are talking
about a combination of both aspects, a synthesis of invention and discovery, of the map and the territory.

Most people today have a rather low opinion of philosophy. They feel it deals with things and problems that are
not real, that do not concern a serious person. They mostly
think of philosophy as questions and arguments about how
the world works, what it is all about. Philosophers themselves call this metaphysics, and curiously enough, a great
many professional philosophers of today and the last fifty
to sixty years feel the same way about metaphysics, that
it is an unreal, useless, and rather silly argument.[33]

The reason for this has been the gradual realization that
philosophy has been based on this division of reality into
two classes, "in here" and "out there," and that this division does not work any longer. It has been useful in the
past. Now it is a nuisance. It just does not fit where we are
today; we have gone beyond it. However, as we are just

developing and learning how to use the new tool, just learning to deal with the concept of our inventing reality at least as much as we discover it, philosophy has largely been "stuck" with the older view, and therefore regarded by the general public and by many philosophers as irrelevant, as a matter of interest only to historians. These philosophers who have dealt with the problems have mostly just criticized the older view and not really developed very much the new one. The research of physicists such as Einstein, Planck, Heisenberg, and Margenau, and anthropologists such as Benedict and Mead, has forced them to see how large was the human contribution to reality and to adopt this view in their work. Nevertheless they have not helped the rest of us very much by exploring, and pointing out to us, the implications for our own life, or by helping us use it to clarify the immense problems we face today.

Many philosophers have, in the face of their discontent with metaphysics, given this area up as hopeless and retreated to just analyzing language. Their idea is that if we can understand language, we can understand all that can be understood. The brilliant efforts modern philosophers devoted to this rather dreary and pessimistic viewpoint have indeed given us some new understanding. The premise it rests on is the in here and out there split. Once we give this up as an outmoded idea, philosophy can return to its former great endeavor of being the attempt, as Kant put it, to determine "what can I know, what ought I to do, what dare I hope."[34]

When Is a Reality "Real"?

V

Do we say then that there is no reality more real, no mode of being more correct, than any other? It certainly seems as if that is where this discussion is leading.

To the question, "Are *all* descriptions of reality equal?" we must answer that they are not, and this negative answer has two reasons behind it.

First there *are* rules and laws governing useful descriptions of reality, although we do not know very much about them as yet.[35] Certainly a description must be coherent; it must not have too many internal contradictions or it will fall apart in our hands. I cannot say that in my description of reality the brain operates like a machine

53

producing thought in the same way a loom produces cloth and at the same time say that the human soul survives death. These are not coherent ideas in a system, they are contradictory.

The second rule we know of for determining if a description of reality is a valid one concerns its ability to reach its goals. Each description of reality, each mode of being, has certain types of questions it is concerned with and certain types it does not recognize as valid. If it is ineffective in answering the questions it recognizes as valid and does not provide clear understanding of how these questions can be usefully answered, it is probably an invalid (not useful) world-picture.

To put this another way, if I can answer the particular questions I am concerned with more effectively in another mode of being, then the mode I am using (which appears to be designed to answer these questions) is not valid. The universe (working combinations of man and reality) is essentially elegant in its nature; it provides answers to legitimate questions.[36] A legitimate question is one a particular organization of reality is designed to answer. If it does not answer its own legitimate questions, a mode of being is invalid.

The simplest example of this is shown in paranoia.If I am seeking serenity, safety, financial rewards, or what-have-you, and if, for whatever reason, instead of dealing with the problems of attaining my goals in a mode of being relevant to them, I organize a picture of reality that includes persecution by the Cardboard Box Manufacturers Association of Minneapolis, I am not going to achieve my goals. Nor will I find ways, in this mode of being of working toward these goals. The same negative results will result if, instead of the Box Manufacturers' persecution, I include secret stores of wisdom from ancient civilizations, the giving up of all responsibility for my own life by letting astrologers or mediums make my decisions for me, or the belief that all my troubles come from things that happened to me in past lives. This kind of organizing will not work in any meaningful way in helping me reach my goals. (It may, however, temporarily reduce psychological anguish and provide a temporary stabilization of my life.) There are other modes of being that will be much more effective in reaching the same goal or goals. For this reason we can say that a mode of being is invalid when it does not answer the questions it purports to answer or solve the problems it purports to solve and another one does these things more effectively.

Another rule of constructing-inventing a valid reality has come to us through long, hard experience. No system that says *everything* is real or everything is imaginary will hold up. Philosophers have been experimenting with these extremes for many centuries, often with brilliance and great intelligence. Some said in effect, "Everything is out there." Others said, "Everything is in here." No matter how much effort they put into these designs, they never were of any particular use.[37] We do not invent or discover reality; we partially invent and partially discover it. Our task is to learn more about this interaction and to learn how free we can be within it.

What other rules there are for designing useful realities, we do not yet know.

This is one reason why we must answer the question, "Are all realities equal?" with a "No." The second reason calls for another shift in the basis of our thinking. As the question stands, it implies a general "Yes" or "No." This further implies that there is one *real* reality or a group of them already existing and that a new invention-discovery of a reality can be matched against these, and then we decide if it is a good one, a real one, or not. This is not the case. There certainly seem to be general rules, but this is a far cry from saying some are more or really real and some are less or not real. We must ask instead, "Equal for what purpose?" We shift the question here to asking if a reality is useful for attaining our goal.

If we decide on a goal, we can then see if the reality we perceive and react to is a useful one to achieve that goal. If it is, we will stay in it and work in it. If not, we can try to design a reality (within the rules of such designing) in which we can achieve this purpose.

A question automatically emerges here. When are you really using a reality, really perceiving and reacting to a specific design of the world? Put this way, the question pretty much answers itself. A reality is real to you when you act in terms of it. Anything else is just talk. It is a valid reality when, using it, you can accomplish the goals acceptable in it. Common sense rules every reality and ultimately decides on its validity.

It is perfectly true you may be wrong, in any reality, about what is helping you attain your results. All scientists remember the example of a concept called phlogiston that was supposed to explain how burnable substances burned. It was a fluid that was released in these substances during burning. Phlogiston was believed to exist for quite a long while and helped explain the results of many experiments, such as the one that showed that ashes weighed less than the substance before its burning. Later scientific development, however, showed that there was no such thing as phlogiston and explained the experiments far better. It is finally true that attaining the results desired by your actions (and acceptable within the reality) are the test of the validity of a reality, but you can make mistakes finding out *what* in the reality is bringing about your results.

If you are concerned about the fact that you can never seem to find a pencil when you need one and that the pencil sharpener always seems to be full of shavings no matter how often you remember emptying it, you might come up with an answer very similar to the phlogiston solution. You might reason that there is a race of unknown beings under the earth and that every night they come stealthily up and grind up all the available pencils in the pencil sharpeners.[38] This explains all the facts, but the idea is wrong. There is no such race of pencil destroyers any more than there is the burnable substance phlogiston. Your reasoning seems valid, but it is based on false premises. As the philosopher Morris Raphael Cohen once said in another context, "You are right from your viewpoint, but your viewpoint is wrong."

Other ideas about how things occur or work in a reality may also be far from the truth. The humorist James Thurber had an aunt who, whenever he was going out in his automobile, would warn him, "Don't drive without gasoline. It will fry the valves." Clearly her idea as to how a car goes differed from others in this reality. I will discuss later some of our present ideas about how things happen that seem to bear a remarkable resemblance to phlogiston, nocturnal pencil grinders, and fried valves.

One thing emerges clearly here. Learning how a reality works, what its laws are, what entities are contained in it, what its possibilities are for attaining the goals it recognizes as legitimate, is a long, arduous, probably never-ending task. We can see this in the slow growth of scientific understanding of the "Sensory Reality," the everyday "common-sense" reality, that is still very far from "complete" (if, indeed, there is a meaning to the term "complete" here; it seems as likely that there is not). This is as true for any other reality. After many centuries of work by some of the greatest minds and personalities of the human race, we are just beginning to understand a little about what we might term the "mystical" (or "clairvoyant") reality. In every reality there is a long task awaiting those who will attempt to plumb its depths, comprehend it, and use it to its maximum effect for attaining the goals legitimate to it.

It is important to be clear about this. A valid reality, a valid mode of being, is not something that can be modified or changed to suit your whim or convenience. It is valid—by this I mean that it works, it is possible to accomplish specific types of goals while using it, and that human beings can survive in it—precisely because it is a clear, definite system of construing reality with its own laws. We cannot play with reality, changing it when we wish. This is not a game of the imagination in which anything goes. You may make up all the schizophrenic fantasy realities you wish but they are not going to work; you can't do anything with them except fantasize about them. A valid reality is a much more serious matter than this. It is a full-fledged, organized world-picture, a unitary metaphysical system, and you cannot capriciously change its laws without losing contact with it. In the sensory reality —the twentieth-century, everyday way of construing reality—there are many things I cannot do and no amount of wishful thinking or loose, soft-headed conceptualizing is going to permit me to do them. The same thing is true in all other modes of being. I cannot modify the flow-process clairvoyant reality of the serious mystic in any way I wish, and there are a great many things I cannot accomplish while using it.

The laws and possibilities of any valid mode of being are very complex and large in number. I do not have to fully understand them to move into a mode. In point of fact, I need to know only the most general ones, what philosopher C. D. Broad called the basic limiting principles of the mode. Starting from these and construing reality in this way, I can start the long, possibly endless, task of exploring reality as construed in this way. Based on the experience of the few modes the human race has worked on in any detail, this exploration takes many centuries of work by dedicated researchers and we have never yet come to the bottom of one of them. Each advance in comprehension of a mode of being permits us to use its potentialities more fully. It took centuries of exploring the sensory reality to develop the x-ray machine in medicine.

Along the way of this exploration, we are frequently wrong in how we explain what we observe while using a particular mode of being. Our beliefs do not make things happen. Our beliefs are part of our choice of which mode of being we use, and things happen differently and follow different laws in different modes, but within a mode things happen as they do and for the reasons they do, regardless of what we believe is the truth. Ice does not stay on the surface of water and not sink for the reason that it cannot push the water aside, even though generations of people using the sensory reality believed that this was the reason.[39]

Changing your organization of reality is not an easy task.[40] We cannot go about it lightly. Even if we stay within one general world-picture—that is, retain the same underlying laws (basic limiting principles)—changing aspects of the way we perceive–react to reality is not easy. We cannot consciously decide to use one mode of being in the morning and a quite different one in the afternoon unless we have really practiced the one that is new for us. It takes a good deal of work, but it can be done.

In the past there have been many examples of how our culture changed aspects of its invention–discovery of reality in order to attain new goals. In the ones I will give here from the history of science, the basic laws of the mode of being were retained and certain limited aspects changed. Despite the fact that these changes were limited, profound differences in our behavior, methods, and accomplishments resulted. (Later in this book I will give some examples in which the basic laws of the construction of reality are also changed and discuss what can be accomplished by this.)

During the Medieval period in Europe, the truth about how the world worked was in textbooks from the past and in personal communications from God. Authority was correct and knew more of the facts than we did, and was to be unquestionably accepted. This was a part of reality and was accepted as such and worked quite well. A tremendous continent-wide plague, known as the Black Death (in addition to various other factors) brought a new problem. Now there was a need to solve the problem of how better to control the environment, how to prevent a recurrence. The Medieval picture of reality was not, it proved, useful for this problem. Over a period of time, the Renaissance, Europeans generally shifted the reality they perceived and reacted to. In the new organization of reality, the one most of us primarily live in today, truth lay in observation and experiment and no longer in historical textbooks or in personal revelation.

We can see one aspect of these two descriptions of reality in the reactions of people to the appearance of a comet. The Medieval man would ask, Why? What is the significance of the comet in terms of man and the process of the total universe? He would look for the answers in the two sources he considered valid: reason, the wisdom of the ancients, and the revelation, direct communication from God. The Renaissance man would ask, How? What is the weight and mass of the comet, and how do these things influence its path and brightness?[41]

The Renaissance reality has worked quite effectively for its original purpose and, on the whole, probably works as well as did the Medieval one for *its* original purpose. It is no more true or false than the Medieval one, except from a biased position that the one you are using is correct and one or the other is closer to it. In deciding which one is closer to truth than the other, we can only be prejudiced.

At the turn of the twentieth century, physical science again had to shift its organization of reality. This time the problem was different and the change had to be much more profound. The scientists had committed themselves to a description of reality that was logical and consistent; it included the idea that all observations had to fit together, to be governed by the same rules. In the course of research, there came up quite unexpectedly some observations that did not fit in.[42] Usually, when this happens, the observations are treated as if they had never been made and are just ignored, or else—as in the minor discrepancies I mentioned earlier—an explanation of them such as the following example is somehow hammered out: "The scientists who made them were lying for their own benefit." This is the sort of thing that has taken place with all the facts of ESP, telepathy and the like. In the case we are talking about, however, this could not be done. The observations could not be ignored and whoever repeated the experiment got the same results. The paradox of a system that demanded consistency and major inconsistent results was itself the problem. To solve it, it was necessary to shift a major part of science into a very different description of reality, a reality in which relationships are more real than identities, in which nothing is separate from anything else, in which all things flow into each other, and in which past, present, and future take on entirely different meanings than they have in our ordinary everyday description. This new description of reality, the Einsteinian revolution or relativity theory, solved the problem of the paradox, but only at the cost of forcing this major change, this shift of description of reality.

We can see these different descriptions of reality in their approaches to a fatal disease. The Medievalist, faced with a fatally ill patient, primarily asked, Why? What did this illness mean in terms of this person's relationship with the plan and goal of the universe? Why were they dying? What did it mean in terms of God's plan? The Renaissance person primarily would ask, What? What were the specific factors of infection, loss of heart muscle tone, stiffening of arterial walls, etc., that prevented the life process from continuing to function? The modern physician would primarily ask, Why does *this* patient have *this* disease at *this* time? What is the totality of this life in which all aspects, sociological, physiological, biochemical, genetic, anatomic, etc., flow into each other, cannot be meaningfully separated, and function as a pattern of which this specific subpattern, the illness, is a part? These three approaches to the problem of illness are obviously quite different and with each of them we will perceive and react to the illness in quite different ways. We can decide which one of them is better for a specific purpose—helping the person to a peaceful death, attempting to restore health, attempting to prevent other people from dying in this way, or what-have-you—but we cannot decide which approach is closer to the truth or is a generally more ideal one. Each of us has a strong prejudice as to which is valid. One of them "feels" right to us, the others do not. This strong feeling, however, tells us nothing about the nature of reality or truth. It only tells us about the culture we were raised in, its beliefs and goals.

From the viewpoint we are exploring, there is no such thing as *the* scientific method. Science is simply the best way presently known to explore and control whatever picture of the universe you are using. Different systems of construing reality will imply different best ways. Classical science (the science of the last century) is refined and disciplined common sense. The laws governing different modes of being differ, the entities in them may differ, and the best way to investigate them differ.

Arguments between science and religion are bound to

be fruitless. In the twentieth century, Western meaning commonly given to these two words, they imply two different realities with two different sets of laws. They also ask different questions. Science today asks only, How? Religion asks, Why? and What? Unless you define first what you are trying to do, what your goals are, there can be no resolution to the argument except disagreement and a failure of communication. If you do make this definition of goal, you can then discuss, with reasonable hope of agreement, the potentialities of each world-picture for achieving this goal and how best to use them in the effort. But, otherwise, to argue from a world-picture based on why and what to a world-picture based on how is like asking if horses or apples are better.

The similarities between these two ways of inventing–discovering reality, science and religion, are very large. Both use a system of defining reality with three parts and study the relationship between them. In science we divide the world into the very small, the subatomic; a middle area, roughly what is perceptible to our sense organs, microscopes, and telescopes; and the very large, interstellar space. In religion it is Hell, Earth, and Heaven. In both we cannot describe in words what happens, except on the middle plane. It leads to the same sort of absurdity to try to describe how a photon can go through two holes in a sheet of metal at the same time without dividing as it does to describe what happens in Heaven. The differences in these two ways include the fact that one rests its case on quantity, mostly spatial distances from millimeters through miles to light years, and the other on quality of being.[43] The two are, as I have said, fundamentally different in that they attempt to answer different questions,

Why? and How? Each will examine certain data and certain problems only, and ignore the data and problems of the other as meaningless or unreal. Each will observe only some parts of what is out there, and will define reality on these parts alone, and will remain in ignorance of the rest. Messages from the universe, as the mathematician Norbert Weiner once remarked, come marked with no more specific address than "To Whom It May Concern." They are only opened and read by those who feel that the message concerns them. Literally, we only ask a question, or see that one exists, when we are ready to listen to the answer.

Science, in our modern usage of the term, is the best way now known to establish an understanding of the conception of the world that will result in prediction and control of what is perceived as out there. It is clearly not adaptable, based on results so far as well as on the theoretical considerations I have been writing of, to problems of human motivation, human relationships—as said before, we can fly to the moon, but not stop killing each other—problems of values and meanings, or problems of the relationship of man to the universe he lives in. To deal with these problems, we apparently need a new conceptual system as much as the Medieval period needed to modify its world-picture in order to control the outside environment.

The Two Writing Desks
of the Physicist
VI

Sitting in my quiet office, I try to be aware of what is happening around me. There is a low hum from the air conditioner in the next room, a gentle scratching from my pen on the paper. The lights are soft and subdued. It is a nice place to work in. Little is, as far as I am concerned, going on in the room and I think and write peacefully. Then I pause and reach across my desk and turn a knob. The room is filled with the roar of rock music that sets my teeth on edge. I can no longer concentrate or even, I feel, survive very long. I turn another knob and in quick succession the room is alive with a news broadcast, a Bach cantata, and a request that I buy a deodorant.

This is a very obvious situation. It does not seem important that I can change a situation by turning on a radio; it is so obvious. The fact itself *is* unimportant; what matters is what it implies. The radio waves were going through the office before I turned the radio on. My limitations, the fact that I cannot perceive them, allowed me peace and quiet. A special translating instrument that changed activity I could not perceive into activity that I could perceive was necessary for me to be aware of the radio waves. The structure of my sense organs determines which part of reality I can perceive and cannot perceive. Here I see clearly how large an effect I have on perceiving–reacting to reality simply because of my anatomy. I screen out a large part of what is going on out there because I can only perceive narrow parts of it. It becomes a clear cliche that I never respond to what is out there, but only to preselected parts of it.

For example, our ability to observe movement is limited by boundaries. We cannot see the hands of a clock move, yet they are moving. They are beyond our "slow" boundary. Any movement that occurs within one eighteenth of a second is also invisible to us. It is beyond our "fast" barrier. Each species has its own barriers beyond which movement is invisible. For example, as far as fast barriers go, human beings are between that of snails (about one fourth of a second) and that of a fish (about one fiftieth of a second).[44] If I had the speed boundaries of a fish or if I had infrared vision or a bat's ears or a Geiger counter or the nose of a dog, or any one of a large variety of instruments, I would be perceiving–reacting to an entirely different reality, as different as the situation in my office before and after I turned on my radio. Which of these realities would be the real one? It depends on my purpose. Which is the real water of the lake? The pure, clear water you swim in, or the active, dynamic life-filled water you see in the microscope? It depends on whether you want to swim or study biology. Both waters are equally real, as is the quite different water a sunfish living in it would perceive-react to, or the water a chemist would deal with. Within the limits of your sensory equipment and your translating instruments, you take one of a set of choices.

There are other sets of choices also. These are not so obvious as the ones listed above. We might go back to the viewpoint of modern physics for a moment. One physicist wrote that as he sat writing about physics he was aware that he sat at two different desks.[45] One desk was the solid, well-used antique upon which he rested his elbows. It was made up of hard, solid, brown, shiny material. This was the desk as he usually saw and reacted to it. The other desk was a shadowy place of occasional energy processes whirling around and interacting in mostly empty space. Occasional stress points of space moved rapidly through vastly greater emptiness. On this shadow desk, his shadow elbows rested. It had no qualities of hardness, brownness, or shininess. In fact, there was no matter in it, nothing but energies; even what are considered the smallest particles of matter, the electrons, did not consist of matter, but only of the energies coming from special regions of space and interacting with all the rest of the universe. (Possibly the best definition of an "electron" is that it is a region of space that exhibits a certain inertia, repels other electrons, and attracts protons. The best definition of a proton is probably that it is a region of space that exhibits a certain inertia, and repels other protons, and attracts electrons!)[46]

The interesting thing about these two desks is the problem of the physicist sitting at it (or them!) writing about problems of modern physics. In order to write he had to sit at the hard, brown, shiny one. In order to deal with his problems, he had to sit at the not-hard, not-brown, not-shiny one. Which was the real desk? Certainly the one he leaned his elbows on. Certainly, also, the problems he dealt with were real, as one can see from our atomic energy plants in operation today: therefore, the shadow desk was real. Was one more real than the other? It depends on whether you wish to lean your elbows on something, or to design an atomic energy plant. You are free to the degree you can shift your reality as you wish to. If you say that only the hard, brown, shiny desk is real, I will ask you to discuss the matter with the relatives of the people who died at Hiroshima and Nagasaki.[47]

Earlier I gave the definition of an electron as a region of space that exhibits inertia, repels other electrons, and attracts protons, and defined a proton as a region of space that exhibits inertia and repels and attracts in an opposite manner. The importance of these definitions should not be missed. Our present cultural reality is not designed to answer questions as to what a thing really is, or any questions beginning with why. It is designed to answer questions as to what a thing *does*, what the interactions of parts and components are, questions beginning with "how to." "What" and "why" questions give, in this mode of being, only circular or silly answers. Perhaps this can be illustrated by what happened when one of the greatest physicists of all time, Clerk Maxwell, tried to define for us, in our usual world-picture, what matter and energy are. He could only come up with the following:

> We are acquainted with matter only as that which may have energy communicated to it from other matter and which may, in its turn, communicate energy to other matter.
>
> Energy, on the other hand, we know only as that which in all natural phenomena is continually passing from one portion of matter to another.[48]

As a matter of fact, the whole question of defining things in terms of "what they are" in our usual world-picture was settled in Athens some twenty-five hundred years ago. Socrates defined man as a "feather-less biped," and the next day another philosopher, who was called for good reason Diogenes the Joker, brought to Socrates a plucked chicken. The ancient Greeks of this period used a world-picture remarkably like our own.[49]

Each world-picture is designed to answer certain types of questions and not others. Those who accuse our cultural orientation of being too concerned with "how to" questions, with being too pragmatic, are missing the entire point. That is what it was designed for, and it is, of course, successful at it and nothing else.[50] If all you have is a hammer, you have to treat everything as a nail.[51] If you want to answer "why" or "what is" questions, you have to find a world-picture organized to answer these questions.[52]

To all this, one particular objection is likely to come to the mind of many people. There seems to be one area of knowledge that is pure discovery and has no invention in it. Mathematics not only seems to reflect absolutely what is in the outside world, but also has the feeling of being true in a pure and above-human sense. This seems to be an exception to the point of view I have been discussing.

Curiously enough, the reason for this feeling that mathematics is somehow a more pure truth than one finds elsewhere lies in the opposite direction from what we would expect. It is the most pure invention area we know of, not the most pure discovery area. In the last 150 years we have found that we could build whatever mathematical systems we like, depending on how we define reality, and all of them—if they are coherently and consistently developed—give us the same feeling of truth. They may lead to completely opposite results and yet each, when looked at by itself, seems to really define what is out there. Mathematicians had, since early antiquity, believed that they were discovering immutable and eternal truths about reality. It was quite a shock when, in the nineteenth century, some of them began to find out that the opposite was true, that they were developing ideally self-consistent ways of describing reality, and that there could be a large number (at least) of ways of doing this that led to completely different descriptions. When the first of these mathematicians started to shatter the old viewpoint, they were frequently regarded as neither serious nor sane. When they persisted and were able to show, for example, that it is just as valid and true to use a mathematics in which parallel lines *do* meet as it is to use the older mathematics in which they do *not* meet, the older approach to mathematics being pure "discovery" was permanently finished.[53] Unfortunately, most of us who are not mathematicians still are holding the older viewpoint and few of those of us who are mathematicians appear to have realized the implications for human life of the newer viewpoint.

It is interesting to note that mathematics, our pure invention, which tells us only about relationships, not about things, leads us to a quite different description of reality than do our senses, which tell us only about things and not about relationships. (The relationships are our contribution as in the example of the melody and the notes referred to earlier.) If we use mathematics consistently we come to the world-picture of modern physics, which is very far from reality as we customarily invent–discover it through the use of our senses. The two pictures of reality, of modern physics and of the senses, are so far apart and so different that we experience a strong tendency to feel one of them must be true and the other false. Alas, for the easy "out" of our human dilemma, experience has shown both to be equally valid. There simply is no such thing as *the* form of the real world.[54] Modern physics is one legitimate description of it, the forms of sensory experience are another. Which is more legitimate depends, quite simply, on what you are trying to do.

Do We Already Know How to Shift Realities?
VII

In order to begin our discussion of how it is possible to shift from one reality to another, let us do a very trivial experiment. Turn on a radio news commentator you like. Now pretend you are in an important examination in a class in speech. Get a pencil and paper and make a mark each time the commentator hesitates in a sentence or stutters. Really concentrate so that you do not miss any. They will be hard to catch, so really pay attention. At the end of the program, write down on your paper what the news was that the commentator reported. If you really paid attention to the test, you will have little or no idea what the news was.

You have, in this little experiment, shifted one aspect of the reality you were living in. What are ordinarily the central and important aspects of your experience became, after the shift, so unimportant that you did not perceive them and, of course, vice versa.

This is, of course, a trivial example. It is only to give you an experience that shifting reality, even a small shift, is possible under your full control.

Most people have had experiences similar to the following. You are, shall we say, dancing with a partner. For most of the dance you are on your usual level of skill doing very well or not so well, enjoying it more or less. During this time your usual consciousness is in operation—you are in your usual mode of being—and you are consciously aware, to one degree or another, of how well you are doing, of how well and what others are doing, of the length of time you have been dancing, how much time is left in the evening, your partner's attitudes toward you, of other people's reactions to you, your level of fatigue, whether or not you would like to sit down for a while, your own anxieties or pride about how you look, and a variety of other thoughts, feelings, self-observations. Suddenly, for no apparent reason to you, the situation shifts. For a period, longer or shorter, you give up all these awarenesses. For this time you simply *are* dancing; you, the music, your partner, and even the others on the floor become one, smooth-functioning, fluid unit. You are, during this period, not even aware it is different, since this awareness would bring us back to the previous state of self-observation and comparisons. You are only fully aware of it afterward. During this time you dance far better than you usually do, you do not lose the beat of the music, step on your partner's toe, or bump into other people. After the period ends, again for no reason apparent to you, you find that you have a sense of exhilaration and good feeling, are less fatigued than when you started, and that you have just had a very good experience.

The same situation has occurred to other people in a wide variety of situations. When playing tennis you may suddenly shift to an organization of reality in which you, the tennis ball, the net, and court are all integrated smoothly and fluidly, when you play far better than usual and do not turn your foot on a pebble or react awkwardly in any way. It seems as if you start moving in the proper direction and to the proper position even before you could know where your opponent will place his return. Again, after it, there is the sense of exhilaration, high energy level, and good feeling. Or, it can happen in a sales situation where your responses and statements have the same special quality and take no thought or consideration but simply *are* and are superbly related to, and effective in, the situation. After a period of this kind, whether you are a salesman, a teacher, a psychotherapist, a carpenter, a lecturer, or a shop steward, you have the good, relaxed but energetic, and pleasant feeling.

Let us look at what has happened here. In your usual mode of being, the usual way you perceive–react to reality, you are primarily aware of the individual, the separate nature of things. To take the tennis example first, there *you* are, holding the *racket,* aiming it at the *ball* to return it across the *net,* into the other *court,* past your *opponent.* Those are six separate objects you are trying to mesh together smoothly. You must hold together in your mind the position of each and, except in the case of the net, count how they are changing. This is a complicated task and requires a great deal of mental effort. Fortunately, or you would not enjoy the tennis at all and would play very badly, you do most of this automatically without being aware of it. (You learn to drive a car in the same way; at first you are aware of all the separate actions you must integrate; then, after a while of practice, you mesh them automatically and your driving becomes a great deal easier and smoother.) The tennis situation, in your ordinary reality, is made up of separate elements because your ordinary reality concentrates first on individual elements, and then on the relationships between them. This is how it works.

When you shifted, changed the way you perceived-reacted to reality, you changed to a reality in which relationships come first and individual elements second. Suddenly you were no longer primarily something separate holding a tennis racket, etc., but were a part of a network of relationships and this came first and the individuality second. It is pretty much the same thing that happened when you took the individual notes the pianist was making and turned it into a melody. (And how much easier it is to recall and reproduce the melody than each of the separate notes in the correct sequence.) The notes did not disappear, but you saw them second to the melody. Here, in the tennis example, you included yourself in the pattern. Once you made this shift of your mode of being, *reality*, everything was different. You no longer had to keep in mind all the six elements and how they related to each other. You only had to let yourself be aware of and respond to the network of relationships of which you were a part. In this mode of being, you, as you afterward realized, moved fluidly, easily, and efficiently, and without strain or effort. The same sort of shift of the way you organized reality occurred in the other examples I used.

So now we have learned something. We have learned that sometimes we shift our mode of being and that therefore we already know how to do it. We may not consciously know what we know, nor—at this time—how we make the shift, but somewhere part of us obviously knows how to do it. We shall now have to learn more about what we do and how we do it. One of our goals is to learn to do at will what we now do from time to time to our own surprise.

As we look at what was going on in the examples in order to understand further what happened, we are struck by one thing about our attitudes during them. In each, the tennis or the dancing or the discussion or the conference, we were only paying attention to what was going on then, at the moment. We were not concerned with or even particularly aware of, all our usual thoughts and concerns: Where is it going and what will the results be, what are the other people thinking of me, how do I look, how do I feel, how long has it been going on, etc., etc. We are very simply and only concerned with one thing at a time. We are concerned with dancing now, or playing tennis now, or stating this point now. This is, indeed, a major shift from our usual way of perceiving and reacting to the world and its relationship to us.

Looking at the same situation from another aspect, we are struck by how we knew something, knew what was going on when our consciousness had shifted from its ordinary way of action. We, in the "unitary" consciousness, did not learn about things in our ordinary way of observing them. We did not just remain in our heads and see what our tennis opponent was doing and figure out how to respond. Instead of observing the flight of the tennis ball, you were, for this time, part of a living network of relationships and reacted according to its flow and its dynamic changes, and according to its overall purpose. As we look back and recall how we were in one of these periods, that is certainly how we seemed to be.

Think, for a moment, about what happens between you and your dancing partner during those moments when you have shifted to this new mode of being. Isn't there a special kind of communication between you? It's not in words and not even completely in nonverbal body signals. Isn't there a kind of almost ESP in which there is communication of the kind of information you are both involved in at the moment? Without thinking about it and without talking to the other person about it, you *know* what the new combination—the one you have made out of the two of you—is going to do. You have completely filled the field of your consciousness with one thing and a new form of perception, of knowing, has appeared. This point will be particularly important when we come to a discussion of how ESP works, happens.

One aspect of the difference, then, is in your attitude. Are you just concerned with what you are doing at the moment or are you, as usual, concerned with a lot of different things? You have to be "one-pointed," focused entirely on one thing to move to this new reality. Recall how a dog who points at a rabbit looks. He is totally focused on it, totally aware of it, apparently there is nothing else in his consciousness, but he is aware of the rabbit and only of the rabbit from his nose to the tip of his tail. And, as long as you are in this one-pointed state of consciousness, you do not separate things, but perceive and react to them as if they were the notes in the melody; as if they, and you, were first a part of the whole, then—and only then—individual. Interestingly enough, although individuality is secondary in this mode of being, it is by no means diminished or lost. To the contrary, it is increased and made richer. The note in the symphony does not become less; it becomes rather more complete and full, clearer and sharper because it is in the symphony than it would be if sounded alone.

This is a strange and unexpected insight we have come to: that from time to time we are able to so shift our invention-discovery of reality that we behave quite differently and accomplish our goals in quite a different manner from our ordinary one. This particular new reality we have been talking about in our tennis, dancing, conference, and other examples has been known of for a very long time as human history goes, and has been widely studied and experimented with and its effects observed.

There have been, for the last two or three thousand years at least, a number of ongoing groups of individuals who spent a great deal of time on this problem. Known as schools of mystical training, esoteric schools, or centers for meditational training, they have explored and worked with the problem of how to affect and change our own consciousness. In particular they studied the shift we have just described, the shift from our usual way of seeing the world first as made up of separate units and then secondarily their relationship to the other way of organizing reality (state of consciousness) in which we perceive-react to a network of relationships first and then secondarily to separate objects.

Mostly, with a few major exceptions, these schools

grew up under religious auspices and with a religious orientation. This was due more to the temper of the times in which they developed than to anything inherent in the work itself. But whether they were set in a Jewish, Christian, Hindu, Buddhist, Moslem, or classic Greek religious setting, or were essentially nonreligious—as are the Zen schools, for example—they were in clear agreement on the major issues: what the shift was, how the world looks after one has made it, how to work at learning to make the shift, and what effect it has on a person to be able to be equally at home in both ways of organizing reality.

Let us take the last point first. There is an old concept among these groups dating back to at least Roman times that gives the flavor of their view on what effect it has on a person to be equally at home in both of these ways of perceiving–reacting to reality. It is the idea that human beings are like amphibians. An amphibian can survive equally on land or in water, but needs both to achieve its fullest being, its fullest potential. So it is with human beings, say these groups. Both ways of being-in-the-world are needed to achieve our fullest "humanhood," our real potential.[55] Further, they all agree, working toward being equally at home in both brings to the individual an increased ability to transcend the negative and painful aspects of life, to function more efficiently, to be more effective in solving inner problems, to have better psychosomatic integration, to live with greater zest, enthusiasm, serenity, and peace.

These claims seem very large, as large as those of modern psychotherapy. However, those who have known people who really worked long and hard at the procedures devised to bring about the ability to shift easily from one way of organizing reality to another report affirmatively: Many of these people certainly act and appear as if they had achieved many of these aims; they appeared to be more fully "human" than the rest of us.

The various groups, whether they are called Yoga, Zen, Christian mysticism, Hasidic (Hebrew) mysticism, Sufi (a Moslem school), or by any one of a dozen other names, all agree pretty much on the type of training necessary to achieve this goal. They all agree that it is done primarily through learning to do one thing at a time and to be only paying attention to that one thing. They may call it focusing the attention, stilling the interior dialogue, coherent attention, one-pointing, bare concentration, or by a wide variety of other names, but they are speaking of the same process. The exercises that they have designed to teach this are called meditations.

A meditation is a tool designed to affect your consciousness much as a gymnastic exercise is a tool to affect your body. Just as different exercises affect our bodies in different ways, so do different meditations affect your consciousness differently.

Both are more than tools, they are disciplines and must be worked with consistently in an organized manner in order to have any meaningful effect. Doing a particular exercise *once* does not have any value other than to give you experience with it. The same is true of a meditation.

I have discussed the theory and practice of meditation, and how to experiment with this discipline and choose your own individual program, elsewhere (*How to Meditate: A Guide to Self-Discovery*, Little-Brown, 1974, Ballantine, 1975) and will not attempt to repeat this discussion here. However, a few general remarks may be in order.

1. Serious meditation is the general discipline of tuning and training the personality as an athlete tunes and trains his body. This basically consists of making the mind as responsive to the will as the body is. It is done by concentrating on one thing at a time, attempting to be as alert and awake as possible with just one thing filling the field of highly alert consciousness. To say that this is very difficult is understating the case. If you try, for example, to simply count your breaths for three minutes, being completely alert and having nothing but your counting in your conscious mind, no other thoughts intruding, you will see what I mean. You will realize that if your body were one tenth as unresponsive to your will as is your mind, you would never get down a flight of stairs without half-a-dozen broken bones. Plato, who knew a great deal about this subject and who, we have reason to believe, was trained in one of the esoteric schools I referred to earlier,[56] wrote that the mind of a human being was like a ship on which the sailors had made a mutiny. They had locked the captain and the navigator below in the cabin. The sailors felt very free. First one sailor, one part of the mind, took command and steered for awhile. Then he lost interest and another took his place. Everyone felt very free, but, said Plato, there was no freedom. The sailors could not agree on a port, a goal to be reached, and if they did, could neither navigate the ship in that direction nor maintain the steady discipline necessary to stay on one course if they found the direction. The task of an adult, continued Plato, is to quell the mutiny, free the captain and the navigator , so that there is the real freedom to choose a goal and work consistently toward it. This is one of the things that meditation is all about.

2. Within the general discipline, there are various paths of meditation. One can use the route of the intellect, the route of the emotions, the route of the body, or a fourth route often known as the way of action. (In this you train yourself through adapting certain attitudes while doing a particular activity ranging from singing to various forms of Japanese martial arts to scrubbing floors, to flower arranging, until the attitudes are reflected in your whole life.) Many schools prefer to combine two or more of these paths in meditational training and, of course, they often overlap. Each of these paths also has subdivisions and special techniques that differ in the different schools, although the basic principles remain the same.

3. There is no one right way for everyone to meditate. Within the general discipline, what is the best way for one person may well be the hardest for another. Just as there is no one gymnasium program that is right for everyone, there is no one meditational program. Each person should find the best program for himself at the present stage of his development. This is done in terms of the individual's own personality assets, liabilities, goals, available time, etc.

4. A teacher can be very helpful in a variety of ways, but is not necessary. There is available enough good written material so that it can be done on your own, although this is harder. However, one must carefully evaluate a teacher. A bad one is worse than none at all. The first evaluation is in terms of what sort of human being he is. If he, and his human relationships, are not what you admire and respect, go elsewhere. If his approach works and he knows it well enough to teach it, it should have worked for him. Then look to see if he is on a "guru trip." If he is, forget him. A teacher should meet

you as a human being, be interested in where you are now, and where you want to go in your development. If his attitude is that he knows what's best for you and what your goals should be and that you should just follow him without asking questions, head for the exit.

5. There is no easy way, no royal road to your own change and development. From the esoteric schools, and from the explorations in psychology and psychiatry in the past hundred years, we have learned that real change is a slow and a difficult process that must be worked at. Anyone who promises you an easy or a quick way is a charlatan. (You might ask them how is it that not Jesus nor Buddha nor Socrates nor, for that matter, Freud, Jung, or Adler, ever suggested growth would be easy. Was it just because they did not know the latest techniques that this teacher is privy to?)

Overall, meditation is a discipline that trains the personality and brings with it more efficiency and serenity. But it also does something more. As we work with it over a period of time, it leads us to a new way of construing reality, to what I will describe in the next chapter as the clairvoyant modes of being. The reasons for this are complex and I do not wish to repeat here what I have said elsewhere,[57] but every school that has worked extensively with meditation has been clear that it develops in us the ability to use these other modes of being, so that what happened to us quite spontaneously in the examples (such as dancing and tennis) that I used earlier in this chapter, we can now do by our own volition and live more and more of our lives in this balanced, "network" state of being that was so efficient and left us feeling so good.

Literally, work at meditation gives us a choice as to the basic way we invent–discover reality. We can then choose which method is most relevant to our needs and problems at the moment. This is, for many, a primary reason for becoming involved in a meditational program.

The General Classes
of Realities
VIII

So far, I have been using the terms "mode of being" and "invention-discovery of reality" and, indeed, the term "reality" itself, without careful definition. It has been necessary first for us to wander around the concept, explore it, and poke at it a little before a definition would have enough solidity and "feel" to it to be anything more than an abstract set of words. To attempt a formula or classification too early in the exploration of a new way of looking at things leaves it empty of meaning for most of us. For this reason I am following a sort of zigzag course in this book, first looking generally at the concept, then defining it more precisely, then looking at some specific areas, such as its usefulness for everyday life and its implications for our social behavior. It now seems time to attempt some definition of these terms.

In order to try to make as much sense as is possible now (with our present limited knowledge) of modes of being, I will start with a description of the general classes these fall into. I will go on to discuss the individual variations within each class, and then describe some of the confusions that occur due to inadequate understanding of a mode of being we are using, or due to mixing up the general classes and using concepts from one of them while we are functioning in another.

We do not, at this time, know all, or how many, general classes of modes of being there are potential for human beings. We do know of four and something of the basic nature of each of these. I will term these the sensory modes of being, the clairvoyant modes of being, the trans-psychic modes of being, and the mythic modes of being.

Each of these classes is a way of structuring what is out there and in here. Each has a clearly defined set of laws and a very great and profound set of implications of these laws. Each is self-consistent, organically organized, and nothing can occur while one is using it that is contrary to these laws and implications. Each of these can enable us to accomplish certain goals and to answer certain questions. Each is irrelevant to certain other questions and goals, and simply does not connect with them. Each has room within it for a great deal of individual variation in the interpretation of the reality and in its implications for behavior. Each satisfies certain parts of our needs, and when an individual does not use one of them with a whole heart, fully accepting its validity and reality, that part of him

remains undernourished and his whole being is stunted in
its development.

The Sensory Modes of Being

Adapted primarily to biological survival, the sensory
modes structure reality with basic attention to defining
differences, boundaries, separations, similarities, and relationships between "things." Essentially, they are oriented toward what can be clearly defined as an entity or
unitary thing, and are adapted to things perceived as out
there rather than in here. They are concerned with separating, contrasting, and defining things in space and time.
Their basic laws (basic limiting principles), within which
all occurrences must happen when reality is structured in
this way, include the following:

1. All valid information directly or indirectly comes
   from the senses.
2. All events happen in space and time.
3. All events have a cause.
4. Causes occur before events.
5. Events in the past can be remembered or—at least
   theoretically—their effects observed, but cannot
   be changed.
6. Events in the future can be—at least theoretically—changed.
7. Objects separate in space are separate objects;
   events separate in time are separate events.
8. All activity—movement—takes place through
   space and takes measurable time units to occur.
9. Action (movement or change of movement) takes
   place only when one entity is in direct contact
   with another.[58]

10. All objects and events are composed of parts that can be—at least theoretically—dealt with separately.

11. When objects or events have similar parts, they can be placed in classes for a specific purpose and the entire class can be thought of and dealt with as if it were one object or event. This can also be done with classes of classes of objects or events.

12. This is the only valid way to regard reality. All other ways are an illusion.

As can be seen from this partial list of basic laws, the sensory modes of being are ideally suited to dealing with objects and events that can be observed with the senses or with devices that, like the microscope and telescope, extend the senses. If you wish to accomplish a physical result—invent an air-conditioning device, raise more food on an acre of land, repair a typewriter, or travel to Paris—these are the modes of being most adapted to the problem. If, on the other hand, you wish to deal with matters completely out of the range of the senses, even with extension devices, you are not going to get very far using it, whether we are talking about electrons or thoughts.[59] You will gain a certain amount of ground by treating these things as if they were within the general sensory range, and then will find that to go further you will have to change the structure of the way you are organizing reality until it no longer fits the basic limiting principles of the sensory modes. When, for example, your data leads you to the fact that electrons move from one position (orbit) to another without crossing the space between them, you realize that you are dealing with a mode of organizing reality that is far different from the sensory modes.

Ideally adapted to asking and answering questions starting with "how" and "how to," the sensory mode is completely irrelevant to questions starting with "why" or to questions of value and moral judgment. It can tell you how to kill or cure, but not which is "right," "moral," "good."[60] It cannot tell you when to kill or cure, any more than it can answer the question of why an object has mass. (The best answers you are going to get to that question are either statements about how much mass it has, statements about how its mass will affect its activity, or if you press hard, the statement that it has mass because it has inertia. If you ask why it has inertia, the answer is ["Right, you guessed it"] that it has inertia because it has mass.)[61]

As with other valid modes of being, however, when used for the purposes it is relevant to, the sensory modes of being function very well in allowing us to accomplish these purposes. The tremendous achievements of science in the past two centuries or so may be legitimately viewed as largely due to the fact that scientists began to use this mode purely in their research. Once they separated it out from other modes so that in scientific research it was used without being mixed with and contaminated by other ways of organizing reality, gigantic strides were made in analyzing large segments of reality, as perceived in this way, and consequently similarly large strides were made in the control and distribution of matter and energy.

The primacy of the sensory modes lies in their adaptation to biological survival. Without them neither a human being nor a human culture can survive very long. An outside threat to the body, or the need to urinate, tends to quickly bring us back to them from any of the other classes of modes we may have been using. The Indian mystic Ramakrishna has said that under the most ideal conditions a person cannot survive outside of them for more than twenty-one days.

As with any other valid mode, the basic limiting principles imply a very great number of specific facts and relationships, potential techniques and their effects, etc., that must be worked out by patient study. It is very similar to the situation in plane geometry where a limited number of axioms, the equivalent of the basic limiting principles, imply a very large number of theorems, the equivalent of the facts and relationships, that can be found if you are patient enough to work them out. It is pretty hard to see the theorems when you just look at the axioms. It is equally hard to see the steam engine and the jet plane when you look at the basic limiting principles of the sensory mode of being. Both theorems and steam engines are implied by, and potential in, the axioms and their relationships in the same way.

The Clairvoyant Modes of Being

The clairvoyant modes are adapted to a direct experiencing of the oneness of all being and process, to the essential unity of the cosmos rather than—as in the sensory modes—its separation into parts, into objects and events. The entire universe, including oneself, is perceived as a "seamless garment" in which *all* divisions and separations, all boundaries, are arbitrary and in error. No object or event can be conceived, in these modes, as separate, isolated, or cut off from the all of being. The universe is one vast flow-process not in space *and* time, but in a unitary space-time continuum, and *is* that continuum. These modes have entirely different basic limiting principles from the sensory modes, and these principles have entirely different implications. To continue the previous analogy to plane geometry, both its axioms and its theorems are different.

The basic limiting principles of the clairvoyant modes of being include the following:

1. All objects and events are part of the fabric of the total of being and cannot be meaningfully separated from it. The most important aspect of any object or event is that it is a part of the total ONE and it is to be primarily considered under this aspect. Considering it under any other aspect is an error.

2. Boundaries, edges, and borders do not exist. All things primarily *are* each other, since they are *primarily* one.

3. This lack of boundaries applies to time also. Divisions of time, including divisions into past, present, and future, are errors and illusion. Events do not "happen" or "occur," they "are."[62]

4. Since no object or event can be considered in itself without considering the all of space–time, the concepts of good and evil do not have meaning. Any application of them would automatically mean the application applies to the total context of being, to everything. The universe cannot be categorized in this way.

5. All forces or situations in space–time, or places where the fields of activity are weak or strong, move with a dynamic harmony with each other.

The very fact of the universe as a flow-process universe means it moves with harmony.

6. One can only be fully in this mode when one has, if only for a moment, given up all wishes and desires for oneself (since the separate self does not exist) and for others (since they do not exist as separate either) and just allows oneself to *be* and therefore to *be with* and *be one with* the all of existence. To attain this mode, one must—at least momentarily—give up doing and accept being. Any awareness of doing or of the wish to do disrupts this mode.[63]

7. Valid information is not gained through the senses, but through a knowing of the oneness of observer and observed, spectator and spectacle. Once this complete oneness is fully accepted, there is nothing that can prevent the flow of information between a thing and itself.

8. The senses give a false picture of reality. They show separation of objects and events in space and time. The more completely we understand reality, the less it resembles the picture given by our senses, by the sensory mode of being.

9. This is the only valid way to regard reality. All other ways are illusion.

These modes are apparently primarily adapted to dealing with processes that are completely out of our sensory range. They are not adapted to biological survival; one would not want to cross a busy highway while using them. Uniting with a truck is not good for you, biologically speaking. At the present time they are mostly used by three classes of individuals or, to put it more correctly, by individuals attempting to attain three types of experience.

These are theoretical physicists working with relativity theory, trying to understand further how reality works; mystics attempting to experience their oneness with the universe; and clairvoyants attempting to obtain paranormal information. (Telepathy, clairvoyance, and precognition are the usual divisions we use to discuss paranormally gained information, information that did not arrive through the senses or from the extrapolation of information that did. Looking at the axioms given on the preceding pages will make it clear that this sort of information is impossible in the sensory modes of construing reality and normal in the clairvoyant modes.)

I have discussed elsewhere the evidence that these three classes of individuals use the clairvoyant modes and will not repeat it here.[64] Suffice it to say, however, that I was able to demonstrate that when relativity physicists and mystics describe the way the universe works from their viewpoint, how they construe or invent–discover reality, it is not possible from the content of their statements to say whether any one of the statements was made by a physicist or by a mystic. They are clearly talking about an essentially identical construction of reality, and it is the same one that clairvoyants say they are using when they describe how reality appears to them at the moment they are attaining paranormal information.

Not only can one not distinguish the theoretical physicist and the mystic by the *content* of their statements (when they are talking about the nature of reality), it is also clear that they cannot be distinguished by the *structure* of their statements. The structure of a statement is a reflection of the structure of the world as the speaker perceives it. It makes no sense in another mode of being.

Take, for example, the following statements, two by mystics, one by a theoretical physicist. They make perfect sense in the clairvoyant mode, no sense at all in the sensory mode:

1. From the Pali Canon, a document of mystical Buddhism:
   Vaccha asked the Buddha,
   "Do you hold that the soul of the saint exists after death?"
   "I do not hold that the soul of the saint exists after death."
   "Do you hold that the soul of the saint does not exist after death?"
   "I do not hold that the soul of the saint does not exist after death."
   "Where is the saint reborn?"
   "To say he is reborn would not fit the case."
   "Then he is not reborn."
   "To say he is not reborn would not fit the case."

2. From Robert Oppenheimer's *Science and Common Understanding*:[65]
   "If we ask, for instance, whether the position of the electron remains the same, we must say 'no'; if we ask whether the electron's position changes with time, we must say 'no'; if we ask whether the electron is at rest, we must say 'no'; if we ask whether it is in motion, we must say 'no.'"

3. From the New Testament, a statement of Jesus:
   "Before Abraham was, I am."

Examples such as these and including statements of the same kind by psychics could be multiplied almost endlessly. Elsewhere I have given an extended series of them.[66]

As with the other general classes of modes of being I am describing here, the clairvoyant modes are adapted to filling part of our human needs and where we do not use it with a full acceptance of its validity, that part of us remains undernourished and unfulfilled. It is our need for a sense, a knowledge, of our solid connectedness with the totality of whatever is, a knowledge that we do not float unconnected in the cosmos but stand firm on the basic rock of the universe. Without this, there is always somewhere a sense of alienation and a need to somehow act to strengthen and cement our anchor ropes to the world. As I shall discuss later, the difficulty is that we mostly attempt to do this in the sensory modes, which are not adapted to the problem, and no matter how hard we try in it we do not succeed and can only continue to try harder in a hopeless endeavor. This tends to evolve to disastrous personal and interpersonal situations.

Certain feelings can only be strong and lasting in us when the part of our nature satisfied by the clairvoyant modes of being is fulfilled. These feelings include serenity, peace, joy, feelings characteristic of the mystic who uses both sensory and clairvoyant modes, certainly not characteristic of the rest of us. Every widespread religion has started with a mystic experiencing and communicating both modes. In its early stages, each of these religions stressed both equally. (The most well-known Western statement is "Render unto Caesar that which belongs to Caesar and render unto God that which belongs to God.") Presently, however, each religion fell prey to the basic statement in all modes of being that it represented the only valid way to construe reality. This usually took the form that the sensory modes were the only valid way (there are exceptions, such as some Eastern groups who opted for the clairvoyant modes as the only valid way), and as the organization of the religion developed in this manner it regarded with more and more suspicion its mystics who attempted to return to both modes as being of equal importance. The statements of the religion as to the necessity of both were less and less heard, even though they were repeated daily. They tended to degenerate into rituals with the full meaning unperceived. (Listen, if you will, to a Catholic Mass with fresh ears, as if you had never heard it before. Explore its meaning as a new statement and experience. Then look around you and see how others in the church hear and experience it. You will see what I mean.)

The clairvoyant modes are adapted to fulfilling that part of us that needs meaning in our existence. It is only when we fulfill this part of us that we can serenely experience meaning in our lives and *know* that we are at home in the universe and that it is a good home for man.

Often we can only see a need clearly when we remove the possibility of satisfying it. Part of our need for meaning is fulfilled by our membership in the human race, in our knowledge of the oneness and ongoingness of humanity, and in our connectedness to the cosmos through it. This is not a thing we are conscious of very much, and as we go about our daily tasks we do not think about it particularly. But remove it and we can feel the difference. Picture, then, a situation in which you *know* that ten years after your death, the entire human race will be sterilized. No more children will ever be born and there is simply no possibility of averting this catastrophe. No matter what task you do or how you *think* you regard it as something purely of the moment, everything would be changed. If you milk a cow, deliver the milk, are an administrator, a writer, an actor, or a carpenter, your work would have undergone a tremendous change for you. The *meaning* would have gone out even though you were never aware it had been there. There now could be no possibility of ever satisfying in this way that part of you that the clairvoyant modes of being enable you to solve. With the sure knowledge of this, life and all its possibilities would be gray indeed, no matter how successful we were at what we had thought was the real purpose of our job.

The Transpsychic Modes of Being

Less is known about the transpsychic modes than is known about the other major classes of modes of being. This is partly due to the fact that in the esoteric schools it was frequently confused with the clairvoyant modes and not usually comprehended as a separate class. The following remarks about these modes are more speculative in nature than the comments about the other three major classes of modes.

In these modes, objects, events, and the self are not perceived as separate from each other, as in the sensory modes, or identical with each other, as in the clairvoyant modes. Rather, they are seen as separate, but flowing into a larger One and with no clear boundary from it. The example of the wave and the ocean has sometimes been used. The wave curling toward the shore is certainly conceived as a separate entity. There is, however, no clear demarcation line between it and the ocean, and the forces and stresses of one affect the other. A similar example might be the arms and legs of the body. Again, they are separate but with no clear separation lines and with such an interplay of needs, supplies, pressures, and forces that they cannot be meaningfully separated. If the arm is removed from the body, the arm is dead and the body maimed and distorted.[67]

In the transpsychic modes, all objects, entities, and events are perceived as related to the total One of the cosmos in this way. Each entity is separate enough to be able to be aware of its own wishes, which is not true in the clairvoyant mode, and connected enough to be able to sometimes communicate these wishes to the total One, which is not true of the sensory modes. This, then, is the mode of being in which intercessory prayer is possible; in which, so to speak, one toe can urge the body to increase its repair systems working on another, damaged toe.

As a further example, one might conceive of a bay of an ocean being conscious of itself as a separate entity and also being conscious of itself as an inseparable part of the ocean. If it knows that another bay is being damaged—say its temperature is becoming higher than it should be—the first bay might, by single-minded force of will, attempt to communicate to the ocean at large the need to bring its immense resources to bear on the problem, to—let us continue this strange analogy—bring from its depth a cooling current.

A famous British archbishop (Temple) wrote, "When I pray, coincidences start to happen. When I don't pray, they don't happen." It is this kind of event we are discussing here. In intercessory prayer, the part (the self, the person) attempts to bring the great homeostatic forces of the whole (the universe, God, nature) to the aid and repair of another part that is perceived as damaged. Usually this is done by a trained single-mindedness of prayer, a total one-pointing of the total part in an attempt to get the signal, the wish, through to the whole.

In the sensory modes, intercessory prayer is nonsense. There is simply no way it can work. In the clairvoyant modes, it is impossible. If I wish for something for you, then already there are two of us and, as this is forbidden, the mode is disrupted and destroyed. If I pray for something for myself, I have also disrupted this mode by (1) separating myself from the rest of the cosmos, and (2) visualizing a future in which change could take place. Only in the transpsychic mode is intercessory prayer reasonable, appropriate, and possible.

The basic limiting principles of the transpsychic modes of being include:

1. Each object, entity, or event is a separate unity, but has no clear demarcation line with the organic integral unity that makes up reality.
2. There are tremendous forces in the cosmos that can sometimes be brought to bear on a local part or situation.
3. These can be brought to bear by an absolute single-mindedness of purpose on the part of one "wave" toward the condition of another "wave."
4. Space is real and "exists" but is totally unimportant. Parts of the whole are separated by it but since they are also connected through being parts of the same One, this does not matter.
5. Knowledge of other parts can come from two sources.

    a. From observation of, as in the sensory modes.

    b. Through being a part of the whole and so perceiving other parts through the whole.

6. From the viewpoint of the individual part, there is free will of each sentient part. From the viewpoint of the whole, all actions that the parts will take are already decided and their results recorded.

7. Since whatever is done to one part affects the whole, an ethical principle is built into the universe. If one part moves another toward greater harmony with the whole, all of the whole—including the part that took the action—benefits. If one part moves to disrupt the harmony (hurt it, damage it, stunt its becoming) between another part and the whole, the disruption affects the all of being, including the part that took the action. Whatever action you take affects you also.

8. Good and evil exist. Anything that moves a part toward its fullest development and fullest integration with the whole is good. Anything that prevents or moves against fullest development of the part and its fullest integration with the whole is evil. In the long run, the terms fullest development of a part and fullest integration with the whole mean the same thing. In the short run, they may not.

9. This is the only valid way to regard reality. All other ways are illusion.

In the transpsychic modes, intercessory prayer of both a positive (good) and negative (evil) nature is possible. In order for it to hold the possibility of accomplishing any results at all, the individual must be using the mode completely, *know* that this is the valid construction of reality. It also takes a complete single-mindedness of purpose where the entire organism or the part is focused on one purpose and nothing else exists in the field of consciousness. This last takes both very strong motivation and extensive training. Given these two, however, it is in this mode that the occasional, very strong miraculous healings (where the healing is beyond the healed individual's own self-repair systems' ability) appear to happen. Whether or not the reverse of such healing, "cursing," also occurs is not clear, but they seem, at this point in our understanding, theoretically to be possible.

Feelings generated by these modes include awe, humility, and a sense of the greatness and holiness of the One that makes up reality. True religious feeling in the sense of awe and reverence apparently rests on the use of these modes. They are irrelevant to the sensory and the clairvoyant modes.

The transpsychic modes are also the basis of the ethical guideline of the Christian "Do unto others as you would be done by," and the Hebrew "What you would not wish done to you, do not do to others." (It was this last sentence that the great Rabbi Hillel said contained all Jewish law. "All the rest is commentary.") In the East, the idea that whatever action you took with respect to others also affected you in the same direction was at the basis of early Hindu teachings. When, however, this point proved too abstract for most people, it was simplified and translated into the sensory modes. There it became the doctrines of reincarnation and of karma: Whatever you do in this life will be done to you in another. This is probably a fair example of what happens when a basic limiting principle or a valid concept is taken from one mode of being where it fits naturally, into another where it does not fit and causes all sorts of logical and semantic problems.

It is in the transpsychic modes that the terms good and evil, right and wrong, are valid, and it is here that we find the moral imperatives and guidelines for our behavior. In the sensory modes these aspects do not apply. An action works or does not work. In the clairvoyant mode, everything is as it should be and again the terms do not have meaning. The clairvoyant modes give us the *reason* for living, the sensory modes give us the techniques. It is the transpsychic modes that give us the guidelines, the ethics and moral structures that give shape to our lives.

The Mythic Modes of Being

The mythic modes of being are the modes used in play, art, and in the dream. They are reflected in the myths and legends of a culture. They have been widely reported in the study of primitive cultures and at one time were believed to be the only reality perceived and reacted to by these cultures. Later study showed that this was far from true. These cultures, as ours, primarily used the sensory modes and often, as does ours, confused them with mythic basic limiting principles and techniques.

The mythic modes are particularly useful in creativity, as they lead to new combinations and to new possibilities of sets of relationships between entities and events. In its own forms and used for the purposes for which it is valid, it is a necessary and effective mode of being. When confused and mixed up with the sensory mode, it leads to such pseudosciences as astrology, numerology, and voodoo.

The basic limiting principles of the mythic modes include the following:

1. There is no difference between perception and symbol, object and image, thing and name. Each *is,* and can be used as if it is, the other. "Objective" and "subjective" cannot be differentiated. There is no difference between in here and out there.

2. Anything can become identical with anything else or stand for anything else once the two have been connected. Once this connection has been made, time and space cannot break it, but an appropriate act of will, correctly expressed, can.

3. Each part of a thing is the equivalent of the whole. If you break up an object or event, each of the parts equals the whole.

4. To control the part is to control the whole. To know the real name of something is to have power over it. To manipulate the symbol of something is to manipulate the thing it stands for.

5. Space is determined by the connections between things and events. If they are connected (and therefore identical) space between them does not exist. If they are unconnected, space cannot connect them. This is irrelevant to sensory space or to geometric space.

6. Time is determined by the connections between events. If two events are the same event, time cannot separate them. If they are unconnected, time cannot connect them. This is irrelevant to clock or calendar time.

7. All events start with a specific act of will. To ex-

plain an event is to show the connection to this act of will which, in itself, needs no explanation and is inexplicable.

8. There is a substance that all things and people have to varying degrees that determines their effectiveness, their ability to influence events. It can be gathered and redistributed by appropriate behavior.

   Its names include "mana," "wakenda," "manitou," "power," "baraka." It is a sort of material "energy" that affects things and determines the course of events. It can be used for good or evil; in itself it is neither black nor white, but gray.

9. There is no such thing as accidental. Everything has meaning and is charged with meaning. Since part and whole are one, to understand the smallest part is to understand the whole and vice versa.

10. Birth and death are a change from one form of existence to another. They are, as are sleep and wakefulness, two similar phases of the same being.

11. This is the only valid way to interpret reality.[68]

Since early Greek times there has been a widespread tendency to explain perceptions and actions made while in the mythic mode by translating them into the currently popular philosophy of the sensory method of perceiving-reacting to reality. Although thinkers as far back as Plato warned against this and pointed out that this was a valid mode in itself, the tendency still continues.[69] The problem here is not that much cannot be learned from this sort of translation, but that its implication always is that the sensory mode is the only valid way of organizing reality and that the mythic mode is somehow primitive and unrealistic.

The crucial aspect of this way of inventing-discovering reality lies in the relationship of what, from the viewpoint of the sensory reality, would be separate objects and events. In the mythic reality, any two objects or events that are perceived as associated are not parts of a larger unity, but are different aspects of it. Each affords a contact with, a hold on, the total. The fingernails of a man may be used to make a doll that will be heated. The man will then have a fever. An Indian peasant woman who is sick will leave on the road a rag she has had bound around the ill part. If someone picks it up, they will have the illness as well as the rag and the woman who left it will have neither. If you change a part of your being in a positive way—a new deodorant, for example—your whole being and your relationships will change in this way. If you wash the knife that gave you the wound, the wound will be clean. If you change your name, you change the course of events that affects you. If you name a new make of automobile after a powerful animal, the car will behave as if it had these attributes and the owner will also have them. The name of an aircraft or ship affects what happens to it. If you treat the flag of a country reverently, you are treating the country reverently. Treat the flag without reverence and you had better watch out for your neighbors. If you were born at a particular time, that time and you are permanently associated. Its characteristics are yours for the rest of your life.

Space and time are filled with the connections of the aspects of unified objects and events and this is their only importance. No distance can separate the man from his discarded fingernails and they are as potent for influence on the man years after they had been discarded as they were immediately afterward. The time of your birth is as potent an influence seventy years after (and two continents away) as it was seventy seconds after you were born. Nothing is objective or subjective; what is, is real. Thoughts, attitudes, feelings are just as effective as actions. Indeed, actions without the proper and relevant thoughts and attitudes are ineffective. Mix this and the sensory reality and you have alchemy. Separate out the mythic reality in the same field of endeavor and you have chemistry.

The value and strength of these modes lies in change, development, and creativity. With anything permitted to be an aspect of, a unity with, anything else you connect it with, all sorts of new combinations are possible. Nothing is forbidden, all relationships are potential. With no holds barred in how you connect things and alloy them, new ideas, insights, and possibilities are infinite. In children's play (and in the play of those fortunate adults who have retained this ability), anything can be anything and new combinations can be arrived at; similarly in the dream. Indeed, it is in play that children train their creative abilities.[70] It is the research scientist, the artist, the writer who has the ability to play with ideas and perceptions who make the real advances and contributions.[71] "My object in life," wrote the poet Robert Frost, "is to make my avocation my vocation." And we know that anyone who succeeds in this will do very well at his vocation.

The necessity for these modes for human beings is seen particularly in two ways. First, it is used in every culture and time we know of. Every group of functioning human beings we know of use it extensively.[72] Second, we can see what happens when we prevent one use of it, the dream. In the dream we use primarily the mythic modes. We now have the technical ability to prevent people from dreaming, but to permit dreamless sleep. When we do this, the person undergoes profound negative personality changes and becomes psychologically quite ill.

When the sensory modes and the mythic modes are mixed together, often quite weird combinations result. Perhaps the most widely known is astrology. The creative value in the mythic modes is shown by the contribution that astrology has made. It has given us the richest vocabulary we have for describing human beings,[73] a vocabulary far richer than that given by the various schools of psychology. However, for the stated purpose of astrology, the predictions of life events as viewed from the sensory modes, it is silly and useless. The concept, valid in the mythic reality, that if you divide a thing into parts each part has all the characteristics of the whole and can reveal the whole, leads naturally to the concept that the Zodiac sign of your birth reveals and is an aspect of your entire life: that once a connection, always a oneness. This is valid in the mythic modes, but completely invalid in the sensory modes in which the events are viewed.

Since, further, everything that is is as real as everything else in this organization of reality, we can see in the combination of the two modes, the source of numerology. A number, in the mythic modes, is not a relationship or a symbol as it is in the sensory reality; it is a thing. And, as a thing, it has characteristics, existence, and more or less of the magical energy that all things contain. Thus, the number three has the most "mana" in most cultures. It is

the unity that separates from itself to make two and re-
unites to make three. Next generally comes seven or nine.
Each number has its own character and own amount of
power. Again this is fine in the mythic modes, but useless
to predict events in the sensory modes.

One reason that astrology and numerology can be
called pseudosciences from the viewpoint of the sensory
reality is that, in the philosopher Karl Popper's words,
they lack falsifiability. They do not include tests that
could prove them false or in need of modification. In this
way astrologers and numerologists are like the orthodox
Marxists who will not accept any possible experience
proving their theory is wrong because, to them, it is right
by the very nature of things. Falsifiability is critical in the
sensory modes in which a thing is valid if it works, has
effects. It is irrelevant in the mythic modes where whatever is, is real.

What in the mythic reality is an attribute of something,
in the sensory reality becomes its way of reacting under
specific conditions. Thus, the inflammability of a body
does not, in the sensory modes, mean that there is a special
substance (e.g., phlogiston) in it, but signifies its reaction
to oxygen; the solubility of a body refers to its reaction to
various liquids under different conditions. What is an
attribute of something in mythic thinking becomes a complex set of relations in the sensory mode of being. This
applies also to the concept of energy. In mythic thinking it
is an attribute. In the sensory reality it is a set of relationships.

In the mythic modes, every action exists on a higher
level of being as well as its own. Playing with dolls is not
just playing with dolls, it is also living out the daily action

of adult behavior. The actions of the adults is a living out of the action of the gods and the myths. Action is given its validity by its being a part of larger patterns of action. An action or event is perceived as meaningless when one cannot perceive the larger platform on which it is an actor, when one cannot perceive the larger script it is acting out. We know, however, that the platform and script are there even if we cannot perceive them.

Nothing is arbitrary in the mythic modes; nothing occurs by chance. Everything has meaning and is charged with implications and power. Things, however, may look arbitrary since it can be hard to trace the connections between the various parts of a unity as these connections, from the viewpoint of the sensory modes, range over objective and subjective, past and future, thing and symbol until they come to that one, arbitrary act of will underlying the whole thing that neither needs explaining nor is explainable.

As the sensory modes tend always to the general, to the understanding of the general laws that underlie each separate event, the mythic modes tend toward the individual. Each thing and event is charged with meaning, is unique and important. The world is full of specialness and newness due to this uniqueness. The child's eye is filled with wonder and possibility as long as this mode is perceived to be as valid as any other. When we teach the child that play is inferior to work, that the mythic modes are invalid, he becomes blasé, the shining newness goes out of things, and the color and possibilities that underlie his creativity are lost.

In play, art, and in the dream we use the mythic modes. With no limitations as to what may be combined with what, the artist ranges freely over the levels and poten-

tialities of being and his new combinations and relationships are often the guideposts for the insights of the
scientist.

Essentially, the mythic modes seem to serve a vital
function in keeping us fresh and alive to the excitement
and wonder of our being in the world. They keep us
interested in our lives, curious, and creative. When we do
not use these modes, we become blasé, bored, uninven-
tive, unmotivated. "All work and no play makes Jack a
dull boy" is an insightful and valid maxim. Anyone who
looks seriously at his or her own dreams (or own play) is
surprised and delighted at his own creativity. The mythic
modes keep the world charged with meaning and as fresh
as this morning's sunrise seen through the eyes of a child.
Without them the sunrise, work, our daily lives, and even
sex is a dull affair.

The mythic modes seem to serve as a sort of psychological adrenalin that prevents the boredom, the alienation, the
anomie of the French sociologists, the *accidie* of the Catholic
Church, which are other names for the apathy and lack of
interest and motivation we suffer without them. Literally,
as long as we are able to play we are never bored. Without
the use of these modes we undergo serious psychological
deterioration—as we have seen in the experiments in
which dreaming is prevented. We can call this deterioration *anomie* and alienation as do the sociologists, *anhedonia*
(the lack of ability to become involved in and enjoy life) as
do the psychologists, or apathy and boredom as we
ordinarily term them, but these are names for the same
thing.

These four classes of modes of being—the sensory, the
clairvoyant, the transpsychic, and the mythic—are the

ways of inventing–discovering reality of which we are clearly aware at this time as necessary for the fullest development of human beings. We must accept the validity of all four and live in them in order to give our total being the nourishment it needs. In the rest of this book I will be discussing various aspects of our potential for each, what happens when we reject the validity of one or more of them, and the effect of this rejection on our personal and social life.

There are probably other modes of being potential for human beings and perhaps even necessary for our fullest humanity. It did take us, remember, a long time to discover that we needed vitamins to survive and we are still engaged in the process of finding out how many vitamins there are. We now know of a number of them we need and suspect there may be others we need but have not yet discovered. The same thing may well be true of general classes of modes of being.[74]

It may be, for example, that the firewalking I described earlier is a sign of a class of modes of being, potential, and perhaps necessary for humanity quite different from any of the four I have described. I do not, at this time, see how the phenomenon could have been produced in any of these four, and so come to the tentative conclusion that it may come from another, as yet unknown, one. On the other hand, however, it may be a phenomenon that can be produced in one of these four when we develop it further. It took a very long period of intensive research into the sensory modes before the possibility of radio and television were conceived. They would certainly have been thought of as magic, that is, impossible in our way of construing reality, a few centuries ago.

There are also other phenomena that may indicate the existence of valid but as yet unknown classes of modes of being. The existence of psychokinesis—the fact that matter can occasionally be affected by willed effort, as Uri Geller "mentally" bends spoons or as in the evidence we have from parapsychology laboratories of similar effects—is not possible in any of these four classes of modes as they are understood at this time. Therefore, it may indicate the existence of another.

These, to me, hypothetical types of constructions of reality may be valid for human beings, and there may be other valid ones also. We do not yet know. I personally lean to the belief that there are, but only future research will give the answers. Leonardo da Vinci once wrote, "Nature is full of infinite possibilities that have never been realized." Who knows what the future can hold for humankind?

I have been writing here of four major classes of modes of being, four ways of being at home in the universe, and of the fact that human beings, to achieve their fullest humanhood, need to accept and use all four. These are a part of our organic needs, and unless we use them all, we leave part of us undernourished and stunted and pay a high price in our development. The next question that naturally arises is: "If all this is true, how much of each of these does a human being need? How much of each do *I* need?"

There can be, I believe, no specific answer to this. Each person is different and his or her needs are different from those of any other person. The combination of the four modes of being that will be most fulfilling for one person will be far from this for another. Each of us must question ourselves and must experiment in order to find the particular combination of the four that is most fulfilling. In addition, there is every reason to believe that different combinations are needed at different periods of one's life.

We are far from any real understanding as to how to precisely answer the question of "how much is needed," except that it is an individual matter and varies for the individual. Our real problem at this time comes long before this question. Our problem at present is to come to grips with the idea that there is more than one class of valid ways to construe reality, that these four, at least, are equally valid, and to learn to experience all four. Only after we have solved this problem can we come to the next one of determining the proper balance of them for each of us.

Within each general class of modes of being there is, of course, room for very great individual variation. In the sensory mode, for example, we can come to major differences in interpretation of facts and in decisions as to how it is best to behave, even though we are structuring reality in essentially the same way. Out of our personal background and our experience we each learn to interpret what we perceive in an individual way and to react uniquely. To this I can only say fervently, "Thank God!" Any system of development that led us all to agree, to perceive and react in an identical manner, would lead to a robotic horror of a world.

There are a tremendous number of variations of the interpretation of reality contained in the sensory modes of being. Although they all follow the same basic limiting principles, they are made different by varying constitutional factors and different experience. They are also made different by varying amounts of accurate and inaccurate information and by varying levels of precise and sloppy thinking. A major factor in the difference is the tendency to mix into our evaluation of reality different amounts of concepts and data from other modes of being than the sensory ones.

We can state, however, that any human individual who biologically survives very long uses the sensory mode. Within that, the man from ancient Egypt perceived reality quite differently from the modern person. And modern people, as we know well to our joy and our sorrow, our gain and our loss, differ tremendously in the ways they perceive-react to reality. The sensory modes indeed give a very wide range for variation within the boundaries of their basic limiting principles.

These differences are also present in the other general classes of modes of being. It may be true, in a figurative way, of those who are also at home in the clairvoyant reality that "All mystics speak the same language and come from the same country"[75] but mystics differ very widely in personality and in their interpretation of what they perceive and how they react in this basic class of ways of construing reality. Mystics are, as a group, certainly in better shape as human beings and nicer people to share the planet with than are those who just function in the sensory reality, but they are by no means identical.[76]

An example of what happens when we try to solve a need by techniques of the wrong modes of being is illustrated by our reactions to the whole problem of personal immortality. From both our behavior and our individual human experience, it is plain that we have both a need for this and a sense, a feeling, that somehow it is true, that somehow we *do* survive biological death. There is, we feel, something necessary about this, that otherwise there is an absurd quality about our experience, our pain, our suffering. Over and over in human history is the record of searching for some solution to the problem.

We try, of course, to solve this problem in the sensory modes of being, by use of problem-solving techniques from this construction of reality. However, the sense and the need come from those parts of us that are oriented to the clairvoyant reality. In this way of inventing–discovering reality, we do survive, we are immortal. This is one reason for Freud's discovery that the unconscious cannot conceive of our own deaths. The unconscious is, at least partly, functioning in the clairvoyant modes of being and therefore *knows* we are immortal, as this is the inexorable conclusion of this organization of reality. (See Chapter 12)

The sensory modes, however, lead just as inexorably to the opposite conclusion. (Chapter 12) In *this* organization of reality we die when our physical brain dies. No matter how we twist and turn in this reality, the results are unsatisfactory. Our actions fail, our reasoning and logic remain faulty insofar as they lead to any conclusion but that of personal annihilation at bodily death. This is the theorem to which the axioms of the sensory reality inevitably lead and there is nothing much we can do about it.

Since, however, the sensory reality is regarded as the only valid reality, and since we have a need of insuring our immortality and a strong sense that this can be done, we— we human beings—keep on trying to insure our immortality in a variety of ways from this mode of being. And we always fail. You cannot twist one construction of reality to reach conclusions foreign to its laws even though, as in this case, the conclusions are native to the laws of another construction of reality. But we keep trying.

We try in various ways. Primarily these are by affecting the groups of others we are in contact with and through having children. Trying to affect the group we relate to, to the degree that we will be forever remembered—that we will continue to affect them, through their memories, forever—leads to some pretty wild and often destructive extremes. One of these is described beautifully in Percy Bysshe Shelley's poem "Ozymandias":

"I met a traveler from an antique land
Who said: Two vast and trunkless legs of stone
Stand in the desert. Near them, on the sand,
Half sunk, a shattered visage lies, whose frown
And wrinkled lip, and sneer of cold command,
Tell that its sculptor well those passions read,
Which yet survive, stamped on these lifeless things,
The hand that mocked them, and the heart that fed;
And on the pedestal these words appear:
'My name is Ozymandias, King of Kings:
Look on my works, ye Mighty, and despair!'
Nothing beside remains. Round the decay
Of that colossal wreck, boundless and bare
The lone and level sands stretch far away."

Another example is of the man from the Hellenistic Greek period who could think of nothing else to do to insure his being remembered forever, and so one night burned down the Temple of Artemis at Ephesus, one of the "Seven Wonders of the World." He confessed immediately the next morning and gave the reason that he wanted never to be forgotten. As a lesser example, there is the story of the poet who wrote a poem entitled "Ode to Posterity." A critic remarked that this message would not reach its destination.

A second way we try to achieve immortality with sensory reality is by having children. Obviously, many factors enter into this activity: the need to love, sometimes the need to celebrate and to fulfill a relationship, economic, social, and other factors, including the fact that human beings enjoy sexual intercourse and children sometimes follow automatically! There is, however, also, on the part of many people, the sense that this gives them a version of immortality. The sensory reality logic of this does not hold up very well. The sense comes, rather, from this being a sign of the parents being one with the stream of the human race and a part of its flow-process. It is correct from a clairvoyant reality participation, but incorrect from a sensory reality participation. It is, however, one of the factors that makes it so difficult to do anything about the population explosion. So long as people do not regard the clairvoyant modes of being as equally valid to the sensory modes, they are going to continue having this particular motivation for having children.

(The complex wills that many people make in an attempt to keep actual control of others after their own deaths demonstrate again the attempt at immortality through sensory reality techniques.[77])

It is interesting to view what happens when we try to

picture what the clairvoyant reality concept of immortality looks like when we try to translate it into sensory reality concepts. It just does not work. Walking on (or floating over) streets of gold forever does not sound particularly attractive. A little better, but basically just as unsatisfying, is the watered garden and the four beautiful girls that a man gets in the Mohammedan version. Even though you are assured the man "never" gets tired of them, or vice versa, it is a bit unconvincing. It is hard to see how *any* sensory reality description of "Heaven" wouldn't get pretty boring after a couple of aeons. Some concepts just do not translate from one mode of being to another. The insoluble problem of immortality in the sensory reality is simply not a problem in the clairvoyant reality, in which "eternity is neither long nor short, it is simply an environment."

The Problem of
Extrasensory Perception
IX

In the first chapter I described the two ways we know that a cultural method of organizing reality is no longer adequate. The first was when major problems appeared that had to be solved, but could not be. The culture's way of organizing reality, its metaphysical system, had been adequate to solve the problems it originally needed to, as the Renaissance system could prevent a recurrence of the Black Death; but could not solve new urgent problems, as how—with atomic weapons in the background—to stop killing each other. When this happens, either a culture must shift its picture of the world to one that will permit the solving of the problem, or else the culture goes under and disappears.

The second way we know a metaphysical system is no longer working is when the exceptions to it mount up. Usually, these are at first as trivial as the examples (the observed shape of a coin, etc.) I earlier described. Slowly, they mount up until they overburden the entire system. When the exceptions, things that cannot be explained in the system, grow to be too many and too clear, the cultural picture of reality begins to break down and make room for the next picture to be developed and accepted.

One of the exceptions that for a long time was regarded as trivial is ESP. ESP refers to the fact that sometimes people have information, often clear and specific information, that they could not have if the cultural picture of reality we have today was "true," was—and this tends to be a fundamental part of any system—the *only* true, real picture of reality.

For a long time ESP was regarded as a silly old wives' tale since—in the culturally accepted way of organizing reality—it could not happen. All accounts of it were believed to be due to coincidence, bad memories, or lies. Since—in the culturally accepted system—ESP simply does not fit in, spontaneous examples (the examples that just "happen" to people) were felt to be so incomprehensible that they were treated as some kind of exception to a solidly known reality and possible explanations just not thought about very much. Experiments that demonstrated its occurrence were ignored or explained as being due to bad scientific methods or to the experimenter's lying. Mainly they were ignored as impossible.

Today it becomes less and less possible to do this. The number of experiments have mounted up beyond ignoring. It is just too clear to anyone who looks at the careful work in this area that ESP does happen. We can run from it, but no longer hide. It has become a problem we *must* solve, but cannot with the old cultural way of organizing reality into what is out there and what is in here.

Let us begin with a few examples:

A. The famous revolutionary patriot of Italy, General Garibaldi, was on the ship *Carmen* crossing the Atlantic on the night of March 12, 1852. He had a strange dream in which the women of Nice were bearing his mother to the grave. He told others about it the next morning. The night of his dream was the same night when his mother died. He had not seen or heard from her for some time.[78A]

B. In the experimental parapsychology laboratory at Maimonides Hospital in Brooklyn, 36 volunteer subjects were randomly divided into two groups. In one group (NG, negative group), their relationships with the experimenter were "abrupt," "formal," "unfriendly." In the other group (PG, positive group), their relations with the experimenter were "friendly," "casual," "supportive." There were two experimenters, each of whom interacted with an equal number of subjects in each group.

Each subject met individually with the experimenter assigned to him for a 15 minute "interaction" period before the experiment. The psychological tone of this meeting was determined by the group to which the subject had been assigned. The subject then completed 200 trials on a machine (a binary random generator) which alternately selected one of two light bulbs as the "correct" one at a very rapid rate (10^6/sec.). When the subject felt ready to make a trial he pressed the button in front of one of the two small light bulbs in front of him. If he was "correct," the machine lighted the bulb corresponding to the button he had pressed; if he was "incorrect," it lighted the other. Whichever one was lit stayed on about a second and then went off. After the subject completed 50 trials, the experimenters would reset the counters, make discouraging comments to members of the NG group and encouraging comments to members of the PG group. Then the next set of 50 trials was started. This was done 4 times until the subject had completed 200 trials.

The basic idea was, of course, to see if the experimenter's attitude would, as predicted, cause subjects in the PG group to do better than those in the NG group. And when the machine's records of "hits" and "misses" was evaluated, there was a real, statistically significant difference in the two groups in the direction predicted. (For those interested I have included some of the statistical data of this study in Note 78B.)

C. A professional man reported to two parapsychologists, some anecdotal examples of the paranormal reception of information which had occurred to him personally. The parapsychologists decided to experiment and test this reported ability to sometimes have information that could not have been obtained through the usual channels of the senses.

In this test, one experimenter drew 90 free-hand drawings (6 in each of 15 sessions). In another room, two closed doors away, the subject tried to reproduce the experimenter's drawings whenever the experimenter pressed an electric switch indicating that she was now working. The target drawing of the experimenter, together with 5 other similar ones made by her at other times, were sent to judges with the subject's drawing separately enclosed.

The judges had no way of knowing which of the 6 experimenter drawings they received was the one that the subject had been trying to reproduce. A careful quantitative method was used by the judges, which scored the similarity of the subject's drawing to each of the 6 furnished by the experimenter. The analysis of the judges' scoring showed that the subject's drawings were much more similar to the drawing that the experimenter was working on at the same time than to the others. ($p.=10^{-7}$). Interestingly enough, there was a statistically significant tendency for the subject to have runs of hits and runs of misses, to be, so to speak, "hot" or "cold."[78C]

D. The famous botanist Carolus Linnaeus (of whom it has been said, "He found biology a chaos, he left it a cosmos,") wrote the following incident. On the night of July 12th, 1765, his wife woke him up shortly before midnight saying that she heard someone walking with a heavy step in his museum. He heard it also and recognized the walk as that of Karl Clerk, an old friend of his. "... I was quite certain that no one could be there, for the doors were fastened and the keys in my pocket. Some days after, I learned that my very faithful friend, Karl Clerk, *died precisely at that hour.* It was certainly his step. I used to recognize Clerk, in Stockholm, merely by the sound of his footstep."[78D]

Here, then, we have four examples of a strange occurrence. People had information that they could not possibly have had, and for each example given here, hundreds just as good or better are available in the journals of this field. Although a paradox, this is a true statement, but it is unfinished. People have had information that they could not possibly have had if the culturally accepted picture of reality—what you and I ordinarily believe it is—were true and the *only* possible way of inventing–discovering reality. The very existence of ESP makes it plain that this is not so.

The next step in our journey is clear. We must ask what way of organizing reality permits ESP to happen as a perfectly normal occurrence. There is no such thing as a paranormal event. There are only events that do not fit into your current system of organizing reality.[79]

Some years ago, I began an investigation into ESP. I started as a complete cynic. The original project was to study the problem of how people I seriously respected—people like William James, Gardner Murphy, and others—could believe in this "nonsense." It was obvious to me that since ESP events were impossible they could not have occurred and these people should know that. In order to understand the problem, I began to look at the evidence. I believed that as a trained specialist in the scientific methods, I would easily be able to see what was wrong with this evidence. To my shock and surprise, I found the evidence very good indeed. Researchers, led by J. B. Rhine, had spent decades in tightening their experimental designs, and no matter how I poked and prodded at their experiments, the result was the same. The evidence was completely solid that ESP did happen.

The next question clearly was, How? The experiments gave no clues here; they simply pointed out that these events happen but gave no idea how. A great deal of effort by serious and high-caliber people had been spent trying to explain ways in which these impossible events might be possible in our ordinary world-picture, but they were all failures. It was clear that this could not be done, at least by me. If these scientists, far brighter and better trained than I, could not do it, I was under no illusions that I could.

However, there is a faith in science that if serious people ask a question for a long time and get no answers, they are asking the wrong question. These men and women had asked, How? I decided to try asking, What? What is going on, what does the world look like, when the impossible event occurs? To my surprise, those who spontaneously, and also under laboratory conditions, had repeatedly been involved in ESP events all answered that it looks quite different than it ordinarily does. This included not only the literate and highly verbal psychics, but also those with much less education and verbal fluency. They said, in effect, that at the moment they were aware of possessing ESP information they were inventing–discovering the world in a far different manner than they usually did. In addition, they all described this other way of organizing reality in essentially the same way.

This was my first introduction to the clairvoyant reality and the reason I gave it this name in my first book on this subject. It was the mode of being in which clairvoyance, telepathy, and precognition naturally and normally occur. (If I were naming it now, I would call it the flow-process reality, or the mystical reality. Clairvoyant reality is not the best term on two counts: First, it implies that ESP occurrences are the most important aspect of this mode of being and I do not think that they are. Second, it incorporates all ESP phenomena under the word "clairvoyance." This is, as the parapsychologist Rhea White has pointed out, an unfortunate use of the word, although I could make a case for it. However, since I have used the name so much, I will stick with it.)

The psychics described the way that the world looked to them at the moment they were aware of having arrived at paranormal information, in a consistent way. They described a coherent, organized metaphysical system, a definite class of modes of being. An analysis of the basic limiting principles of this class of modes of being showed that when using it, ESP is as normal as it is paranormal when using the sensory modes of being.

Earlier I described "your space"—the space in the reality you are now using—as just large enough to contain and separate all the objects you react to as real and existing now. "Your time" similarly is just long enough to contain and separate all events you react to as if they are real, whether or not you perceive them as existing now.

The problem of ESP is that it involves interaction between entities—people and people or people and objects—that are separated by space and/or time. In the examples I gave earlier, it is impossible, in our usual reality, for the people to have had the information they clearly had because of this separation. Paradoxes such as this are unacceptable to common sense. (Also they are uncomfortable, which is why most people and most scientists have done their effective best not to think about them very much.)

The problem is that space or time so separated the two entities involved that communication between them was impossible. Yet, communication occurred. Space and time, however, are defined as just large enough to separate all entities you perceive as separate. Suppose you shift to a reality in which the entities are not seen as separate, but simply seen as parts of a larger, total, single entity (as when you shift from considering the separate notes to considering the melody). In this case, when you shift to a reality in which the two entities involved are now the same entity, your space automatically shrinks so that it is no longer separating them. There is no problem of communication between them. Similarly, with time, when you make the shift it automatically shrinks so that it no longer separates entities and so that you no longer perceive-react to them as separate. The problem of ESP has disappeared.

And this is apparently exactly what happens when ESP occurs. When I questioned those people who are frequently involved in ESP attainment of knowledge, sensitives or clairvoyants or psychics, on how the world looked to them when they were attaining ESP information, they replied by describing the clairvoyant reality. This is a reality in which no two entities are separate because everything flows into everything else. With no separate entities, time and space shrink until they can no longer separate anything.

One of the factors that make ESP so difficult to produce and maintain consistently in the laboratory begins to emerge into light here. This is the fact that as soon as we *try* to do something, we are involved in a world-view that involves present and future, doing instead of being, and a difference between the self and others. This is the sensory reality in which ESP is impossible. The clairvoyant modes in which ESP is normal do not contain these possibilities. If you try, you are disrupting these modes. It is almost impossible when working in a research study on ESP not to try to get results, and as soon as you do you are making it impossible. The line that must be walked between being oriented toward and trying is, indeed, a razor's edge and subjects continually fall off it. It is no accident that the most successful, recent laboratory experiments in ESP have involved techniques that first modified the subject's consciousness—through dream states, hypnosis, meditation, restriction of stimuli input, etc.—in such a way that the conflict over being in a study involving ESP and not trying to obtain results was lessened.

The problem of the paradox of ESP seems solved by our concept of different valid realities. It is apparently true that many sensitives do not shift deliberately, or with conscious awareness, to the clairvoyant reality, but are only aware afterward that they had momentarily shifted. (This is similar to the dancing or tennis examples given earlier, in which we were only aware of having shifted realities after we had returned to our usual one.) We can, however, train ourselves to make this shift consciously and deliberately and then perceive-react to a world-picture in which ESP is the natural way to attain information. I have described elsewhere my own experiences in training myself and others to do this and the successful results.[80]

It is clear that the flow-process, ESP reality (the clairvoyant reality) is one attainable to human beings if they are willing to work at the process. A certain percentage of people, with a type of personality organization we do not yet understand, seem to shift into it nonvolitionally and unpredictably from time to time. These people, however, also improve their ability to do this with training or self-training.

It appears that the paradox of ESP cannot be solved without the concept of alternate realities. Without this concept we are forced to recognize that impossible events happen (as, for example, in precognition when someone has information about events that have not yet happened, and that could not be figured out [extrapolated] from presently existing information). We know that this happens and that, in our culturally accepted sensory reality, it could not happen. In this reality an effect cannot occur before its cause. But this is exactly what happens in precognition. Apparently the only way out of the dilemma is that there are other, equally valid ways of organizing reality, and that one of these was being used by the recipient of the information.[81]

Although disbelief in ESP, in the paranormal, was once considered to be good, modern science and a holding to the scientific viewpoint, it is now the remnant of a long-outmoded view of science. If you say, "ESP cannot happen, therefore it does not happen," you are also saying, "I believe absolutely that every event, without exception, can be explained on the basis that the universe runs like a great machine and that *all* events have a specific cause." This is a view of eighteenth- and nineteenth-century physics, but far from the view of the physics and science of the twentieth century. Today we believe that other systems of explanation must sometimes be used. On the subatomic level, that *statistical* explanation must be the way we account for events; on the level of life forms, an *organizing* quality must be the explanation of such behavior; and on the level of the very large, as in interstellar space, or on the very fast, as in approaching the speed of light, *field-theory* explanations must be used. The person who denies the possibility of ESP on scientific grounds is, indeed, expressing the view of the best scientific thought of 1875.

One aspect of this is the gradual shift in modern thinking from the concept of cause to the concept of information. One system or being is no longer seen as causing another system or being to act. Rather, the new view is that the first system provides information to the second, which receives it, interprets it, and then acts in accordance with its entire nature and history.[82] The concept of DNA, the information principle in genetic transmission, is probably the best-known example of this change in scientific thinking.

It is indeed strange that those who hold against the possibility of ESP on the grounds of "rigorous scientific views" find, if they care to look, that these grounds have moved on and they are upholding a banner that science has long deserted in its forward movement. In the words of one philosopher: "A man who marries the spirit of his age soon finds himself a widower."[83]

Modes of Being and
Everyday Behavior

X

Perhaps the single most important thing that I have said so far in this work is that *all systems limp.* No way of describing the world, no world-picture is complete. All leave out a part of what it means to be human. If a mode of being provides nourishment and fulfillment to one part of our nature, it leaves out, disregards as unreal, other parts. Each system, furthermore, includes as one of its major premises the concept that it is the *only* valid way-of-being and that the others are not valid. We are constantly tempted, therefore, to accept only the one system we were raised on and thus to feed only a part of our being. In human history the other parts almost invariably remain undernourished and wither.

132

This seems to be one reason, perhaps the major one, that human beings have nearly always acted in such sick and self-destructive ways. Always unsatisfied and unfed in parts of our being, always rejecting those parts as inferior or unreal, always believing that our way was the only right way, we have turned in our agony on ourselves and our neighbors, filled with blind panic and anger like rats in a poisoned cage. The price for rejecting a part of oneself is well known in the human sciences of both the psychodynamic and of the esoteric schools. This price is anger against the self, self-loathing, anger against others and, at bottom, a blind rage against the universe, which, we feel, forced us into this position. The self-hostility and hostility against others are always acted out in some way and these ways run the gamut of our illness from the need to fight wars at least every twenty years, to scapegoating (surely there is *someone* we can blame our anguish on), to psychiatric and psychosomatic illnesses. *No one* who feeds only part of his being escapes unscathed.

The strange, sad part of all this is that we know, as human beings, how to shift to different modes of being in order to nourish and satisfy different parts of our being. The child knows how to shift easily into the mode of being we call play (one of the mythic modes), and knows how important and how real this world-picture, this way of perceiving and reacting to the world, is. Further, every child knows the difference between the play mode of being and the sensory mode of being. What the child takes a long time in learning, and what often gives us the impression that he or she cannot tell the difference between the two modes, is that adults consider only one of these two world-pictures as valid and real, the other as inferior and unreal. It is this error that takes the child so long to learn, and when he learns it finally, he bids good-by to the child within himself, to his lifelong cost, regret, and sorrow. How much we respect those adults who have retained the ability to play and who have maintained contact with that wonderful childhood ability of immediacy, of living fully in whatever they are doing at the moment, of the full ability to be doing one thing at a time, of the joy and wonder and infinite possibilities of the world. How much we respect these adults, and how hard we try to train these abilities out of our children by teaching them that play is inferior to work and that the play mode is inferior to the sensory mode. No wonder we see dimly the bitter truth in the statement of the wise psychologist Max Wertheimer that the definition of an adult is "a deteriorated child." The statement has just enough truth in it to make us wince. Those qualities that come from being free to live in more than one mode of being and so come closer to our full humanness are the qualities that we have lost and that we see ourselves, willy-nilly, training out of our children.

It is not only in the wonderful play of childhood that we see ourselves somehow knowing the importance of using other modes of being and knowing how to shift to them. When we listen to music and are in it so completely that we abandon the sensory reality and we and the music are One, and that One is all of reality that exists, we have shifted to another mode of being. Whether the music is Mozart or rock is of less importance in this context than our shifting modes and our knowing how to do this even though we do not consciously know what we know. In every culture we know of, music has been of great importance to many people. It is one of the great routes left to adults to feed an otherwise unfed part of their being. Our culture teaches us what kind of music to respond to in this way and permits us this avenue to being more completely human, to expressing and satisfying another part of our needs; and usually also teaches us, unfortunately, that this other part is inferior to the part satisfied by our particular cultural world-picture, and can be satisfied only when our day's work is done, only when we have lived primarily in the culture's definition of reality.

There are other ways also in which we show our needs for other states of consciousness than the one our culture has decided is the only valid one. There is the telling of tales, whether it be the storyteller squatting in the bazaar with an enthralled crowd around him, or the evening television program. Here, too, we have relegated the part of our nature this feeds to a second-class citizenship. We tell our children that it is to be kept for the story hour and that this will appear only if the child has been good, that is, if he or she has satisfied first the requirements of the sensory reality. In television we patiently endure the same message; we only hear the story if we listen to the commercials, which occur whenever the story gets so exciting that it threatens to bring us completely into the reality in which it exists.

There are a hundred other ways we seek to live other modes of being and to nourish our starving parts: with alcohol and drugs, with the single-mindedness of complete abandon to "senseless" violence, in giving ourselves to prayer so completely that "here and now cease to matter," in the oneness with the universe that can be produced with the thunder and vibration of the racing motorcycle, with the identification of ourselves with something larger than ourselves, whether this be a professional football team or a nation. The important aspect of these behaviors in this context is not so much whether they are healthy or unhealthy from any particular point of view, but that they show we have a variety of ways to shift our mode of being, how naturally fluent we are in this process, how each culture, to survive, must provide a number of areas for doing this or else be destroyed by the anguish of its citizens. We are naturally experts at this shift but, I repeat again, trapped by the belief of every system that only it is the valid way of being, that only its picture of reality is the real one, and that all others are unreal, invalid, and not to be engaged in except at those special moments when we have fulfilled our tasks in the *real* world and are resting for our next round of these tasks.

So deep is this implication in each world-picture of its exclusive rights to the territory of reality that we sometimes even see specialists in changing their own modes of being fall into this trap. I have written earlier of the esoteric schools that train individuals in moving from the sensory reality into the flow-process, field-theory, clairvoyant reality. If anyone knows much about the subject of there being more than one mode of being potential (and necessary for fullest humanhood) in each human being, it is these schools. Yet, many of them, particularly in the East, sooner or later fall into believing that the clairvoyant reality, the world of the One, is the only real reality, the only valid mode of being, and that the sensory mode of being is inferior and invalid. Losing their original goal of widening human participation in the universe by teaching choices in how to define it, they retreat to the same narrow view they started from, with the only difference being a different definition of what is the one valid way of perceiving–reacting to the cosmos.

I mention this here only to point out again how strongly implicit in each world-picture is the idea that it is the only real one. Each of us has this belief to a greater or lesser (generally much greater than we know) degree about the sensory reality. It is terribly difficult to accept that other modes of being are just as valid for their purposes, just as necessary for our human nature, just as fully a part of us as the sensory reality, and that they can be ignored and unfed equally at our peril.

We do not ask ourselves why every culture that survives one generation has its artists and musicians, its storytellers, and sagas. We do not ask ourselves why it is not only the new, unfamiliar story that is preferred, but, equally or more, the old familiar one. The characters and their problems may or may not change, but the world it is in, the reality it defines and brings us into, is the same. We prefer the familiar story we have heard a hundred times before, or the type of music we were raised on, because we can easily shift into its world-picture, and this is what we need more than the new and unexpected. It may be one knight or another, "without fear and without reproach," battling evil sorcerers or dragons in a world-definition where these can exist. It may be one television detective or movie spy or wise physician or another of each of these, but we know the strange rules of the universe they inhabit. We know that right and justice—in this other world—will always triumph after facing almost insuperable odds, and that no matter what the disastrous situation, the forces that be—God, science, the author, the playful child who produces and directs—will, as in our myths and legends and as we did in our childhood play, bring about victory. We know that death and defeat are permanent for the evil forces and temporary for the good. Both the good Sherlock Holmes and his evil enemy, Professor Moriarty, might have fallen together into the deadly Reichenbach Falls at the end of the first series of stories, but it is only Holmes who returns alive at the beginning of the second. In each action, in these tales of heroes and detectives, we repeat the great mythical themes found in every society from Ulysses to Perry Mason. And, for a little time, we live primarily in the mythic world-picture and so renew and refresh another part of our being.

There is another way that we demonstrate that we know how to shift our mode of being. A mode of being is, remember, a metaphysical system, a map of reality that describes it as containing certain things and working in certain ways, having certain laws. Sometimes we show by our behavior that we have shifted without knowing consciously what we have done. We frequently do this when we are reacting to the reality around us as if it contained some different things and contained some laws it did not seem to have, as judged by our behavior, a short while before.

A mariner finds his boat has been left stranded on the shore as the tide receded. He looks up in a book a table of high and low tides that tells him exactly when he can expect the next high tide that will float his boat. Then he waits with more or less patience for the time to pass. Since he has sufficient sensory reality information to deal with the problem, he continues to use this model of reality and his perceptions and reactions conform to it.

The same mariner, on his now-refloated sailboat, is some weeks later becalmed at sea. There is no wind and he does not have sufficient information to predict with any accuracy when the wind will again start to blow. He is, therefore, likely to shift to the mythic mode of being without being aware of it. Indeed, he would deny it or laugh ruefully at himself if you pointed it out. His behavior, however, shows this shift. He may whistle for a wind, put his hat on backward, invoke one or another class of nonhuman helpers by praying or in some other way. Although he is not aware of what he is doing—and, if pressed, would say these are merely "superstitions"—he acts as if the world now was constructed on quite different lines than it was when he was stranded on the beach and did not even think of whistling for a quicker high tide. And it is our actions that show how we are inventing–discovering the world.

It is a trivial example and yet it can show how easily and naturally we can shift our conceptions of reality. If my car stops running in the middle of a deserted country road, I will first see if I have enough data in the sensory reality to fix it in this mode of being. Since I know little about cars, this testing will probably consist of tapping the gas gauge to see if it has gotten stuck and reported an empty gas tank as full, opening the hood to see if there are any loose wires I can notice, and possibly removing the gas feed tube and blowing through it to make sure it is clear. (This last once actually worked for me!) If none of these procedures suffices, I have then run out of sensory reality information with which I can deal with this situation in this mode of being. Without noticing what I am doing, I then make a shift to another reality system. I may kick the car several times as if it were a stubborn donkey I could persuade to move in this way. I may promise it a complete motor tune-up and perhaps even a new paint job if it will only behave. Presently, I may threaten to sell it to the nearest junkyard unless it behaves and gets going *this minute.* And so on. In my frustration over not being able to use the sensory reality satisfactorily I have, unawares, shifted the entire way I construe reality and my behavior shows this. I have behaved exactly like the natives of the Trobriand Islands. When they go on a routine fishing expedition where they know the problems and solutions, the variables operating, they are only concerned that their canoes, paddles, and fishing gear are in order. When they are going on a more hazardous trip where they do not know all the variables involved, they add incantations, magical rituals, and amulets.[84]

Again, this is a trivial example, but it shows a way to explain some of our behavior in more serious situations. How often do we make the same sort of shift in interpersonal or social situations? How often have we tried to deal with a problem involving our relationships with another person or group of persons in an "intelligent," "sensible" manner—that is, by using our data from the sensory reality—and when that did not solve the problem, changed our behavior—shifted, unawares, to another mode of being—and tried to handle the difficulty with the interpersonal equivalent of kicking the stalled car or the balky refrigerator? If we look at our newspapers or history books, we become immediately aware that many of our attempts to deal with interpersonal or international problems start "sensibly," start by using the best data and techniques from the sensory reality. When these fail, as we do not have enough information on the subject (as our becalmed mariner had insufficient information on what produces wind and what the relevant conditions are) we shift to "irrational" modes of behavior; that is to say, we shift to actions based on a completely different way of defining human beings and the universe. I will explore this point in more detail later and look at some social situations, and what we can learn from this concept about constructive ways of dealing with them. For the moment, however, it will suffice to look at our main solutions to the problem of international tension. We cannot, for example, seem to resolve the fact that both we and the Russians fear that the other will suddenly attack with atomic weapons and destroy us. Both nations know they have everything to lose and nothing to gain by a war. The very concept of a major war between atomic powers is an idiocy and we know it. We have tried to deal with the problem on the "sensible" level of the United Nations, discussion, increasing international trade, summit meetings, etc. Since we do not have enough information to do this successfully in the sensory reality, we—in part only, thank God—have resorted to a technique that is, from the viewpoint of the sensory reality, quite irrational. The technique is to constantly increase the amount of retaliatory weapons as if "more than needed" could do the job when "as many as needed" could not. I do not know the number or potency of the rockets we and the Russians have aimed at each other at the time of this writing. Sometime ago it was enough to destroy every human being on the face of the globe eleven times over. From the viewpoint of the sensory reality, it is completely clear that if this number of weapons was not enough of a deterrent to prevent each side from attacking the other, no larger amount of weapons would do the job either. It is clear that if you have "enough" weapons, it does not matter if the other fellow has "more." If you and I both have pistols aimed at each other's head, there is no reason for me to be concerned if you are holding a cocked hand grenade in your other hand. You can't kill me twice. And yet, both we and the USSR continue to pile up more bombs and delivery systems and show by our behavior that we have shifted to a different system of organizing reality from the one we were using before, are unaware of this shift, and still believe we are using the old one. And the new one we have shifted to does not work, is not adequate to the problem of our mutual fear and distrust.

It may well be that, as has sometimes happened in the past, a shift of our cultural way of organizing reality will occur and the problem will not exist in the same, incredibly dangerous, way in the new cultural mode of being. At one time in our history, the conflict between Christian and Mohammedan segments of humanity seemed unsolvable. The best that could be attained were occasional periods of exhaustion when neither had the energy or organization to try to militarily overwhelm the other. The change in the way reality was organized known as the Renaissance made this particular problem obsolete and it eventually simply dropped largely into historical records only. Similarly, in Europe at a later time there seemed no way, given the reality as it was then organized, to solve the Catholic–Protestant conflict. Again a change in the perception of reality made this conflict obsolete. It may well happen that the same thing will occur in the communist–capitalist conflict but we had better not hold our breaths waiting for it. The stakes are simply too high. Perhaps, however, if we look carefully at the concept of our creating–discovering reality, and the concept that we can have some control over this process and can organize our construction of reality in ways that can solve the problems we face, we may be able to design realities that can save our planet.

Social Conflict and
Modes of Being
XI

Human beings live primarily in the sensory reality. This is so and has always largely been so since these modes of being are constructed on a basis of effectiveness, of biological survival. There is no problem with this fact, or would not be, were it not for the additional fact that the sensory reality includes the premise that it is the only valid reality. Despite the secondary channels to expression of other modes of being left open in all cultures, major parts of the human organism are left unfulfilled and undernourished. As I have written earlier, the part of a human being fulfilled by his being in a particular class of modes of being are only fully satisfied when the individual recognizes this class as a valid one. As long as it is seen as inferior and secondary, the needs of the particular parts of us it is needed for are left unsatisfied.

One part of us that has long been recognized by the esoteric schools and by all major religions is the part that needs to know we are not separate from the whole, that we are an integral, inseparable part of the universe. I have called the construction of reality that satisfies this part the clairvoyant reality and have described it earlier in this book.

Its essence is a view of reality that is one total process with all parts, including "ourself," organically related and integrated. Each entity or unity in this view is so much a part of the total and so impossible of meaningful separation that it was possible for various mystics to try to sum it up by the statement, "All is one." There is, it appears, a spectrum of ways of organizing reality along this dimension that ranges on the one extreme to a complete individuality of all entities (without even meaningful classes to consider them in), to the opposite extreme, a complete oneness of everything. As human beings we need perception and expression at both ends of the spectrum, not just one; of both the sensory and clairvoyant constructions of reality.

Our need to perceive and react to the One end of the spectrum is shown in countless ways in our behavior. The most typical way is to so modify our perceptions that we see larger groups as ourself and perceive that whatever is happening to these larger groups is happening to us. Politically, this has—see any history book—disastrous consequences, but before I write about this aspect, it may be easier if I start with a brief discussion of baseball and football teams (read soccer, cricket, or what-have-you for other countries).

We choose a team made up of interchangeable players who, from time to time in their careers, will probably play for other teams. We may admire the particular player, but we emotionally relate to one team, no matter how its composition changes. We rejoice when it wins a game or a "pennant"; we are depressed when it loses. We are not a stupid or a silly species; this behavior must satisfy some real need in us. The answer seems to be that we have a need to see ourselves as part of something larger than what is inside our skin limits, and that this behavior satisfies such a need. The sports teams solution is not new in Western culture. The Byzantines in the seventh century were as deeply involved in the Green and Blue chariot teams as Brooklynites ever were in the Dodgers baseball team.

This sports identification is an interesting and useful attempt at solving the need, but one look toward our general behavior shows it is not enough. One cannot solve a need by giving it inadequate fulfillment; all you can do in this way is to sometimes ease the pressure a little. There is an experiment with white rats that shows a fascinating parallel. You put the rats on a salt-free diet and then put a tiny amount of salt in their drinking water. The amount of salt is just large enough to be perceptible to the rats, but too small to ever fill the need. The rats will drink and drink, become terribly bloated, and continue to drink until they literally drink themselves to death.

It is much the same case with us. We—being inventive and creative beings—invent all sorts of ways to solve the need, but it is never enough and can never be enough, since we do not recognize as a valid need with a valid solution, the modification of consciousness. The most common form of group we invent is a political form: tribes, cities, and nations. The problem here is again that it eases the need, but not enough; and so we keep on with the equivalent of the rats' water drinking. We use a technique every child quickly learns for strengthening the group and for increasing our involvement in it, for increasing the intensity of our feeling of being a part of it. We find an enemy. When an outside force threatens a group, each member becomes a much-needed part of it and knows this. His sense of himself as an integral and organic part of the group intensifies. He sees himself more as the note in the symphony rather than the individual note. This is clearly more satisfying than the weaker identification we have when no enemy threatens.

I use the word "clearly" and the evidence is plain. We behave like a species that *needs* to fight a war every twenty or so years, and continue to behave in this way when there are simply no more possible excuses we can find if we are creatures who are built to live only in the sensory mode of being. We know we have nothing to gain by war, everything to lose, and simply cannot stop.

It is interesting to note that we do not even have, in our culture, an explanation of our continued involvement in war that holds together when we examine it. Wars have been fought by groups of men living under a very wide range of social, economic, and cultural conditions. It is easy enough in examining the history of each war to find the exact series of circumstances that led to it: the angers, the fears, the complaints, the clashing interests, the broken treaties. However, as the historian Thucydides warned us long ago, we must look beyond the specific events if we are to understand the real causes of even a single war. How much further, then, must we look behind the specific events if we are to understand the problem of war in general? Not to ask, "What events led to the outbreak of this war or that one?" but rather to ask, "What is there in man that makes him so ready to go to war almost no matter in what culture or under what economic conditions he lives?" The question we pose here concerns the readiness, the receptivity, the seed-bed on which the specific events fall and which, when nourished by it, flower into intergroup conflict.

The basic question set forth is thus that of wars in general. They are a fact of human behavior: very widespread, easily stimulated into being, terribly difficult to prevent or control. Whether raised in a tribe, a city, a state, or a nation, man frequently engages in this activity. Whether rich or poor, single or married, in democratic or authoritarian societies, in rigid or flexible cultures, he gathers in armies and fights other armies. What is there that gives the energy behind this behavior? Why does he do it?

The question appears either naïve or overwhelming. Either we feel that it is ridiculously obvious and simple to answer, or else that it is so complex that it is impossible to deal with in any useful manner.

It may be worthwhile to start by examining the answers our culture has given, historically and in the present, to this question. At the same time we will ask if these answers are in accord with the orientations and knowledge of the social sciences today. In this way we shall see if the reasons for man's apparently almost universal readiness to go to war are already known and, if so, what, if anything, we can do with this knowledge. If the answers we have are *not* acceptable in the light of modern scientific knowledge, we shall have to look further and try to see more clearly.

There appear today to be three major groups of answers to our question. For purposes of discussion we shall label these "Psychological Theories," "Economic Theories," and "Social Group Theories." Let us survey each one briefly.

Psychological Theories

Psychological theories as to man's readiness to go to war are very old. In the Greco-Latin world it was widely believed that all men want power; that no matter how much power they have, they want more; and that this desire must inevitably lead to wars. The surprise with which classical authors report exceptions to this—see, for example, Herodotus's discussion of Otanes, who did not want to be king of Persia—shows the strength of these beliefs. "Love of power," says Thucydides in his *The Peloponnesian Wars,* "operating through greed and through personal ambition was the cause of all these evils." Other forms that psychological theories have taken is that man is born evil or that he is genetically and basically a carnivore. The basic concept of man is akin to that of the philosopher Hobbes. In this viewpoint there is something in man's nature that naturally leads to large-scale, overtly aggressive action against his fellows.

On a much more complex and sophisticated level, Freud stated his belief that because of an instinctual death drive that must be externalized if the individual is to avoid destroying himself, nothing can be done to stop war. The best we can do, said Freud, is to await the time when mankind progresses further in evolution. In an exchange of letters Einstein asked, "Why war?" and Freud answered, in effect, "Because man is what he is."

Obviously, if there is an inborn need in man to fight wars, there is little that the scientist can hope to do about prevention. He is helpless against an organic part of man's nature. Let us, however, first look at this concept and its relation to the present viewpoint of the social sciences. We may accept this view as children of our culture; do we also accept it as scientists?

Instinct theories of molar human behavior are not generally in good repute today. We would question the validity of an instinct for power, an instinct for aggression or murder. (Similarly, most social scientists would question the existence of a Thanatos, a death instinct. Even in psychoanalytic circles, this concept has not gained wide acceptance.) Further, and more importantly, the *behavior* of social scientists clearly indicates that they do not believe in the psychological theories of war. An industrial psychologist acts to reduce hostility within a business organization. A social worker attempts to prevent hostile activities among juvenile gangs. A psychotherapist helps an aggressive patient to find a way of living with other men without overt and violent conflict. None of these seems to believe that in so doing he is acting against the basic nature of man. It therefore becomes clear that present-day scientists do not believe that man has something within him that must lead to warlike activity or to war itself. They act in ways clearly opposed to psychological theories of war. Appealing then as the concept is that it is inherent in man to fight wars, we must reject it. It is too clear a contradiction to the behavior of our social scientists.

Economic Theories

The economic, the "corn and iron" theories of the basic causes of war are also very old. Livy, the Roman writer, writes of Tarquin's preparing for war against Ardea: "Their wealth was, indeed, the reason for Tarquin's preparations. He needed money." Thucydides, in ancient Greece, tells of the Corinthians urging their neighbors to join them as allies in a war to protect their import–export trade. In this view, man fights for wealth, he goes to war to obtain the goods and possessions of another.

It is obvious that since the Industrial Revolution at any rate, and beyond question since World War II, the economic theories of war make no sense at all. The bald and unmistakably clear fact is that war destroys more capital and personal goods than the victor can hope to take from the loser. To try to explain the present international political tension on the ground that those involved believe war will increase their wealth, is obvious nonsense.

(In a nomad culture, the economic theories may be valid. In a non-nomad culture, they are not. However, there have been no nomad cultures of importance for a long time.)

Shall we go further and hypothesize that wars once increased wealth (or seemed to) and that we continue to have them either out of habit or as a sort of "phantom limb," leftover behavior pattern from the past? The habit hypothesis does not appear to be tenable. Our present knowledge assures us that habits, per se, do not continue in the absence of motivation.

The "phantom-limb" hypothesis is a more difficult one. It assumes that men continue to believe what was once true because they have not successfully re-evaluated the problem. We know that this occurs in many situations. However, *this* error, the idea that war does bring profit, appears to have been clear to many leaders, both political and intellectual, at least in the last century. It has been repeatedly demonstrated to the public of the world. Where we might once have accepted economic gain as a possible motive behind war, we can do so no longer. This class of theory also must be rejected. When a man can produce so much more wealth as a worker than he can gain as a soldier, it simply does not make sense to regard economic gain as a powerful force driving toward war. Whatever its effect in the past, it is no longer a reasonable explanation.

Social Group Theories

This group of theories all appear to contain three basic elements: first, that human beings exist in groups (a necessity of their nature, economics, early conditioning, or for some other reason); second, that the behavior of groups is quite different from the behavior of individuals; and third, that inherent in the structure of human groups is overt intergroup hostility.

That human beings are group-organisms, and that the behavior of groups may follow quite different laws than does the behavior of individuals, does not seem germane to our inquiry. However, the concept that groups are not only inevitably hostile to each other but must express hostility between them shows a great number of exceptions (e.g., the United States and Canada). More to the point, however, is the difference with which we treat small and large groups. On the small group level we do not act as if we regard intergroup conflict as inevitable. On this level we act rather as if we believe that the prevention of overt conflicts and the solution of covert conflicts are legitimate and reasonable goals of the social science. Active group work, psychotherapy, city planning, and various techniques from industrial psychology are among the many tools we use in achieving these ends.

It is only on the international level that we seem to have regarded their overt aspects as inevitable and inexorable, and have not organized major research programs that might enable us to understand them more deeply and to ascertain whether through greater understanding some action could be taken toward control.

One is startled if one compares the time and energy expended by social scientists in research on understanding and reducing the aggressive components in juvenile gangs with the time and energy spent by social scientists in research on understanding and reducing the aggressive components of nations. The contrast, particularly at a time when the nations have atomic and bacteriological weapons, and the juvenile gangs do not, is striking. We are forced to the conclusion that, in these theories, a nonverbalized assumption exists that aggression is *not* organic to members of small groups, but *is* to members of large ones. This assumption does not appear to be an acceptable one. Therefore, we cannot accept this group of theories as the answer to our question. It would involve us in too fundamental a paradox.

These three groups of theories include the major answers that our culture has given to the problem of man's readiness to fight wars. On consideration, we see that none of them is acceptable. They have formed part of our cultural assumptions about the basic causes, but either logic or our behavior as social scientists forces us to reject them as satisfactory solutions. We shall have to admit our ignorance of this tremendously important and basic problem and try to approach it with a fresh mind. What we have been doing in this survey is to examine our assumptions and have found that they need, at the very least, much further testing and refinement.

Very often in man's consideration of this problem, he has confused the stimuli, the specific events, that led to war with the problem of man's receptivity to these stimuli. Thus, for example, Herodotus reported the view that the long-term, destructive Greco-Persian conflict was caused by a series of kidnappings of women. That specific events, or the drive for power of a leader, or a psychopath in a position of authority, or the psychological illness of a Hitler or Stalin may serve as the specific stimulus that sets a war in motion, is not questioned here. Rather, we raise another, and what seems to be a more basic question: that of man's willingness and readiness to respond to these stimuli. Why does he follow the trumpets? It may be that in this seemingly almost universal condition, we shall, if we can understand more about it, find the type of knowledge that will help clarify some of the forces behind our history of repeated, armed, intergroup conflict.

If the three solutions our culture has for its war behavior are not acceptable ones today, is there another? I believe that in the approach to reality I have been describing in this book, there is a fourth solution. It is that war is an attempt to solve a set of our needs, the needs that mystics and others who meditate seriously solve by moving into that construction of reality I have called the clairvoyant reality, or the clairvoyant mode of being. This need is the need to know one is not only a separate individual, but also an inseparable part of the total family of being. This theory would fall flat if mystics also tended to identify with baseball teams, cities, or nations, but quite obviously they do not. They tend rather to identify at the least with all mankind and, more usually, with all life. Certainly, they behave as if such were their identification. They have filled a set of needs by knowing that the clairvoyant mode of being is a valid one and using it to the degree they need. They then show by their behavior that they have no further need to identify with cities, nations, or football teams, and no need for scapegoats, enemies, or wars. The logical interpretations from this appear to be clear.

The Problem of "Survival":
What Happens to the
Personality at Bodily Death
XII

The essence of this book is that human beings have more and wider choices than we have generally known. Within limits we can define the relationships between "ourselves" and "reality" and define what we mean by these two terms. We have a choice of realities to live in and the ability to choose a definition of reality that will most suit the problem and the needs we are dealing with at the moment. Each of the general classes of modes of being has its own axioms and theorems, its basic limiting principles and inexorable results arising from these.

The differences between these general classes of modes of being cannot be overstressed. In each of them the basic definitions of "man" and "reality," "in here" and "out there," are different, as are the definitions of such fundamental categories as "time," "space," "causation," "creation," "annihilation," "matter," "energy," and "existence." In each, different things are normal and paranormal, possible and impossible. Their similarity lies in the fact that they are all valid invention–discoveries of reality. Beyond that they differ and their solutions to problems differ.

It is the last phrase that is particularly relevant here and particularly hard to comprehend. Our mind boggles at the idea that a problem may have two different, contradictory or equally valid solutions (let alone more than two!).

The problem is not a new one by any means. It was that great genius, St. Thomas Aquinas, who first perceived that there could be completely different valid approaches to a problem, approaches with very different methodologies built into them. He demonstrated that the "rational" and the "irrational" ("reason" and "faith," the senses and "revelation") were both valid approaches to the problems he was dealing with. What he could not perceive, however, was that they did not always lead to the same solution. His faith in the rationality of God—and therefore of His creations—was so strong that he believed that even if one approached reality by nonrational means, the answers to the problems would be the same as if one approached it by rational means. This led to one of the most intense debates of the Medieval period. Aquinas's opponent, Siger of Brabant, believed that there could be different, often contradictory, valid solutions to a problem that was approached in different, but valid, ways. Aquinas strongly disagreed.[85] The Medieval Age definitely awarded the victory to St. Thomas. Today we would be less certain. Most of us would still feel that a problem can have only one valid solution, and if approached by different valid methods, would still yield it. Others among us would remember such questions in physics as the problem of whether light travels in waves or particles and the solution we have had to come to: It depends on your method of studying light and what you are trying to do. We would recall that from the viewpoint of relativity physics, whether two events occurred at the same time or sequentially—and, if sequentially, which one occurred first—does not necessarily have only one valid answer, but various ones depending on the observer's frame of reference. That whether or not parallel lines ever meet depends on the geometry you are using. We would recall the explorations of Freud, Jung, and Binswanger, of anthropologists such as Benedict and Mead, and philosophers such as Ernst Cassirer and Morris Raphael Cohen. We might recall examples such as the maps described earlier in this book and a great many other examples and explorers of what is. We might then wonder if, in our modern view, we would award the palm to Aquinas or to his opponent.

Clearly, from the viewpoint of this book, and, I believe, from the viewpoint of today's science and thought, there is, for many problems at least, more than one valid solution. Literally, there is no "way the world works"; it works differently if you structure it differently. This, however, if comprehended does not leave us in chaos. It leaves us with choices we can make.

One of the great questions of concern—at least from time to time—to every thinking person is the question of "survival": what happens to the personality when the body dies? We all feel that there *must* be one true answer to this question and that all other answers, no matter how arrived at, are untrue. And if there were one way that the world works and the correct method of thought would lead us to understand this, our feeling would be correct. What we have been finding out in the past hundred years or so, however, is that this is not so; that there is no way things are, but at least several different ways that we can construe them. We have been finding out that there is no privileged metaphysical system that gives us the true answers any more than there is a privileged geometry that gives us the true answer to the problem of parallel lines ever meeting. The anser to the problem of survival rests on the way we organize, invent–discover reality. Different ways of doing this lead to different answers.

What is essential here is that these different answers to the problem are not just verbal or intellectual answers. They are not word games. They are the real, the true answers. If you use a particular, valid mode of being, that is the way the universe really works. The solution to a problem implied by a valid reality is the real solution. It is what happens. When we change our use of one general class of modes of being to another class we are changing reality, not just our viewpoint. Reality is now operating with the axioms and laws of the new class of modes of being and what occurs normally under these laws is what *does* happen. In one geometry, if you actually draw the parallel lines far enough they really intersect. In another geometry, they don't no matter how far you draw the lines. Under one type of experiment light does not appear to travel in waves. It does travel in waves. In another experiment it does travel in particles. In one coordinate frame of reference, Event "A" happened before Event "B." In another frame of reference, they were simultaneous.

One of the most dramatic instances of this arises from certain relationships worked out in relativity theory between time, mass, and motion. In its simplest form it goes as follows. Two twins are born in London on a particular date. They are clearly, give or take an hour or so, the same age. One twin, Joseph, remains in England all his life. However, on their twentieth birthday, the other twin, James, enlists as a deckhand on a spaceship making a very long trip. (This story will have to take place a bit in the future, but we have excellent reasons for supposing the important parts of it are true.) The spaceship travels at 99 percent of the speed of light for part of its journey. Fifty years pass in England—Edward XI is now on the throne—and the spaceship returns to earth. The brothers have a reunion. Joseph is now seventy years old, but James is only thirty-five. It is not only that he thinks he is thirty-five or looks thirty-five. He *is* thirty-five and only thirty-five years have passed since his birth. Seventy years have passed since his twin Joseph was born. There is no one answer to the question, How many years have passed since the twins were born? There are two true, real, different answers to the question. One twin is thirty-five years old, the other twin is seventy.

It is not our view of things that changes when we change major classes of modes of being, any more than it was only our view of how old each twin was that was so confused. It is reality, which is always a combination, a synthesis, of what is and our invention–discovery of it,

that changes and brings about even greater differences between different classes of modes of being than arose in the
strange tale of Joseph and James.

It is true that within each general class of modes of
being we have much less freedom. In each we are working
under a definite set of axioms and theorems, of basic
limiting principles and their inexorable implications and
we cannot go beyond them, cannot violate them. Things
only are and happen in accordance with them. We can,
however, change the class of modes of being we are using
and therefore automatically and normally have an entirely new set of inevitables and impossibles, be in a new kind
of reality with very different entities, laws, and solutions
to problems.

What has all this to do with the problem of survival? As
with all the great questions, this has different solutions in
different classes of modes of being. The mode of being you
are using will determine the answer to the problem. And
the answer—and this is the hardest part for us to comprehend—will be the true answer. What is normal, inevitable, in this class of ways of construing reality will
actually happen. The solution is a real one, not just a
verbal or theoretical one.[86]

"This is all very well," one might answer, "but supposing that this is all true and that different classes of
modes give different valid answers to the problem. You
have said yourself that the sensory modes are the ones
adapted to biological survival and that we must live primarily in them or die. What are you suggesting? That we
give up the sensory modes because we don't like their answer to the problem of survival and thereby stop sur-
viving?"

It certainly appears to be true that the different classes of modes of being give different answers to the problem of survival. (I shall be exploring what these are in a moment.) It is also true that we cannot give up the sensory modes. They are primary for our biological life. This particular problem, however, is not a real one. Once you emotionally and intellectually accept the equal and full validity of the various classes and practice them sufficiently, you *automatically* use each one for the relevant situations and needs (sort of the way an experienced traveler, at home in several languages, operates as he travels across Europe, or a trained musician plays in whatever key the music demands). You do not have to worry about which one you are using at a particular moment. You use the one that suits your purpose. ("Suits your purpose" here refers to both the problem you are dealing with at the moment, and the inner needs to nourish that part of yourself that is fed by this particular class of modes of being.)

What answers to the problem of survival are given by the various classes of modes of being? I have discussed in detail elsewhere the answers of the sensory modes and the clairvoyant modes and will only repeat them briefly here.[87] The implications of the transpsychic modes and the mythic modes have not, to my knowledge, been worked out sufficiently to enable us to do more than speculate about them.

The Sensory Modes of Being and Survival

In this reality, a thing is real (exists) if one or more of three, often overlapping, conditions are true:

1. If we can directly perceive it.
2. If we can directly perceive its effects.
3. If we must believe in its existence in order to account for effects we can perceive but cannot account for in any other way.

In other words, nothing is real unless it is perceived or is necessary to explain a perception. The perception may be in the past, the present, or the future (as the interest we expect to perceive when our deposited money has been in the bank long enough). If a thing does not fulfill any of these three reasons, it does not exist in the sensory reality. Everything that is real has effects. (It was under this criterion that the famous Michelson Morley experiments were interpreted as proving that the "ether" did not exist.)

In this reality, a thing ceases to exist when it no longer fulfills one of the three conditions. When the bulb is turned off, the light it gave ceases to exist. It did exist as long as it was perceptible and had effects. Since it no longer does these things, it no longer exists although we may remember it.

The self-awareness and consciousness of other people is considered to exist because, partly on the basis of our experience with ourselves, it is the only way we can explain the behavior we observe in them. It exists since it fulfills the third condition. It is a "construct," something we cannot observe, but which must exist to account for something we can observe.

However, by the rules of the sensory reality, it only exists so long as the behavior exists. When this ceases at biological death, then these same rules make it cease to exist. The consciousness and self-awareness of a person who has died no longer exist, as they no longer fulfill any of the conditions of existence of this Reality. In the sensory modes of being, annihilation of the consciousness is the inevitable result of the ceasing of activity that accompanies biological death.

The Clairvoyant Modes of Being and Survival

In the clairvoyant reality, a subpattern is considered to exist if it meets *all* of three conditions:

1. It must be necessary to complete our view of reality. Its absence must leave an inharmonious gap in the relationships that make up being. It must form observations (or comprehensions) into a harmonious relation with the rest of the One. If they do not fit in this way, they are irrelevant to the One, and since this includes all of being, this means that they do not exist.

2. It must be the simplest and most elegant subpattern we can make and still fit our observations into the total One.

3. It must mesh smoothly and inexorably into the One and function according to the same laws that govern the whole. To the degree it does this, it is valid (real); to the degree it does not, it is invalid (unreal, nonexistent).

In the clairvoyant reality, the self-aware, conscious "I" of ourselves and others is a valid subpattern under the first two requirements. It is the simplest construction we can make of a strong set of comprehensions. It is also valid under the third requirement *if* it is conceptualized within the rules of this reality. This means that it is perceived as being without boundaries in the continuum, as not being separated from or isolated from the rest of "what is," not being bounded in time or space; in other words, if it is conceptualized in the clairvoyant mode of being.

This is the central point. The sensory reality *geometrizes* the universe in terms of boundaries, separations, lines, and surfaces. Boundaries and limits are inherent in the structure of reality. A lake is bounded by the land around it; a life by the terminal points of birth and death. The opposite is true in the clairvoyant reality in which no part can be legitimately separated from the rest and in which boundary lines and points do not exist. The independent particle does not exist but is part of the total field.[88] Instead of "This too shall pass away" there is "What was, is, and shall be." Events do not occur, they *are*. The subpattern is not separated from the rest of the total field of being by space or time. Consciousness is not limited by death since this would be an illegitimate boundary line. The clairvoyant reality leads as inexorably to personal, self-aware survival of biological death as the sensory reality leads to annihilation.[89]

This is the reason that the great religions have been so traditionally concerned with the state of consciousness at the moment of biological death. From the Tibetan chant for the dying, "Nothing to hold to, nothing to do," to the Christian rites, they try to bring the dying person to a clairvoyant mode of being at this moment to insure his or her survival. Many people do this themselves as death approaches. Everyone who has had extensive experience with the dying has seen those who, as the ceasing of biological functioning approaches, move into a serene, transcendent state of consciousness that is frequently a state that they have never experienced before. Shakespeare wrote of it as "a merry. . .lightening before death," and it is a beautiful and inspiring thing to be present at.[90]

"But come now," one might well reply. "This all sounds very well. It is logical and follows from your argument. However, it is plain silly. Let us take the example of the monk who is meditating and is as deep as one can get into the clairvoyant mode of being. A meteorite falls on his head and crushes it. Chop logic and words all you want, he is no longer alive. That is the end of him. Take one look at his mutilated body and where is all your argument?"

It is certainly true that the monk is dead; dead, that is, from the viewpoint of the sensory reality. When we judge from this viewpoint as to how reality is constructed, death, the end of being, occurs when the body ceases to function. However, the whole thrust of this book has been that this viewpoint is not *the* valid way to construe reality, but *a* valid way to construe it and there are other, equally valid ways. From the viewpoint of the clairvoyant reality, with its impossibility of absolute boundaries and edges, with its "What has been, is, and will be," the monk is not dead. Observed from this mode of being, he is alive. And this viewpoint is as valid as that stemming from the sensory modes.

Further, it is not just the mode of being at the moment of death that is important. Here, I believe the religious techniques that attempt to bring the dying person to the clairvoyant modes of being are engaged in a double procedure. First they are trying a last–ditch, final attempt to bring the person to this mode to insure his survival. Secondly they are attempting to relieve the anguish of dying. If it works, bringing the person to this mode at the last minute, fine. It would seem, however, far more intelligent to try to become familiar and at home with this mode at other, earlier, and less stressful periods of life. This, if the argument is valid, is all that is needed as "once" you are in this mode, then—from the viewpoint of the sensory reality—you are "always" in it.

The basic answer to the problem of the monk and the meteorite, however, lies in the construction of reality from which you are trying to answer the question. If we judge the problem from the viewpoint of the Sensory Reality, the monk is dead. If we judge it from the viewpoint of the clairvoyant reality, he is not. There is no one right answer. As we have repeatedly seen earlier in this book, as, for example, in the case of the twins Joseph and James, there may be more than one correct answer to the same question and these different answers may be equally true.

The physicist Henry Margenau in reviewing this question has raised another point. He asks whether, freed from the input and impediment of the sensory reality, the clairvoyant (or even the transpsychic and mythic) modes of being might not more fully unfold themselves. I must confess that I am very much struck by this observation and that it appears convincing to me.

The Transpsychic Modes of Being and Survival

To my knowledge, the implications of the transpsychic reality for survival of biological death have not been worked out in detail. It appears to me likely that this reality leads to a nirvanalike state in which the consciousness of the individual is merged with the consciousness of the whole, but I do not know of sufficient exploration of the matter to be able to speak on this with any certainty.

The Mythic Modes of Being and Survival

Again, I do not know any answers here. I am unaware of any detailed work that would tell us what happens in the mythic modes at biological death. In these modes, as we shall see later, the concept of "spirits" is valid, but I do not know if, in this reality, survival as "spirits" is possible or normal and inevitable.

The problem of survival, then, appears to be related to the mode of being you are using. Your state of consciousness determines what happens to your consciousness at biological death. Literally speaking, your survival or your annihilation are up to you.

Curiously, this is not, for most of us, a pleasant answer. We would prefer, somehow, that there was only one answer to the problem, and that it was inherent in the way the universe worked and that it was not up to us. We are, perhaps, made uncomfortable by the responsibility implied by this solution.[91] However, if you wish to take as much control as possible over your own destiny, to be more and more free, this approach to reality gives you the opportunity. You can work with your consciousness to develop skill in other modes of being than the sensory ones. It is up to you.

The Concept of Spirits That Intervene in Human Life
XIII

One source of many problems we run into as human beings is our tendency to mix up the general classes of modes of being. Generally, this is related to the fact that we only regard one class as a valid way of perceiving-reacting to reality and so all events, problems, and needs have to be explained by and dealt with in this particular construction of reality. At best this leads to all sorts of logical and language problems. At worst it leads as we have seen to self-hatred and conflict within the self and to hatred for others and violent conflict between people. One area in which there is immense confusion due to the confusion of different classes of modes of being is in the concept of spirits that intervene in human life.

We might begin this discussion by looking at a curious contradiction in modern science. This involves one of the most sacred of the sacred cows of science, the second law of thermodynamics.

Before you decide (unless you have training in physics) to skip over the next section as incomprehensible, let me say that it is a very simple law. It merely says that unless you do something about them, things get less and less organized. Your kitchen utensils start off well organized in the proper drawers, but unless you keep putting them back in place, they tend to get spread all over the kitchen and eventually all over the house.

A different example would concern the point of a knife that you hold in the gas flame. When you turn off the flame, the point is very hot, the blade moderately hot, and the handle is cool. Everything is well organized in a complex system. Now the second law begins to operate. Gradually, the entire knife becomes the same temperature as the heat diffuses through it. The point becomes cooler, the handle warmer. Then the heat diffuses farther and the entire knife becomes the same temperature as the room. The room becomes the same temperature as the rest of the house and so forth.

The second law of thermodynamics certainly works for knives, houses, and the sensory reality in general. However, the sensory reality is adapted to events and objects within the range of our senses, or the range when it is extended by such devices as microscopes, telescopes, or hearing aids. The sensory reality is not adapted to ranges below and above these, to the very small (as electrons, etc.) or to the very large (as galaxies or clusters of galaxies). It is for the explanation of events occurring in the very large ranges that relativity physics has adapted what I have called in this book the clairvoyant mode of being.

Now back to the second law of thermodynamics. From its success in the medium-sized systems where it is very useful for physicists and engineers, scientists have generalized it to the very large, to the universe as a whole. They have pointed out that it means that the whole universe is "running down" and will eventually die what has been called a heat death. This simply means that the heat in the universe now concentrated in certain spots (as in stars) will gradually diffuse and spread out until the universe is no hotter in one place than it is in another, in the same way the heat at the point of the knife spread over the entire knife. Similarly, the atoms of matter, like the kitchen utensils we spoke of, will gradually diffuse and form less and less complex and complicated combinations until they, too, are equally spread out over the total universe. At that point—fortunately, unimaginable aeons in the future—no place in the universe will be different from any other, nothing will be happening, and if anyone were to be still around, he had better go find a new universe. In this universe, the entire neighborhood will have gone to hell!

This theory of a second law of thermodynamics eventually running the entire cosmos into the ground is generally accepted in physics. It comes from small systems we observe in the sensory modes of being.

However, when we go to large systems beyond the range of our senses, the sensory mode is not very useful. Here the clairvoyant modes are more applicable. These lead, at the present stage of our knowledge, to two major theories about how the universe works. It is these theories that are generally accepted, if constantly argued over, in science today. And neither of them follows the second law of thermodynamics and neither of them includes the concept of a heat death.

These hypotheses are generally known as the big bang theories and the steady state theories. In both of them, things get more complicated and more highly organized rather than less. One, the steady state theory, starts off with simple atoms of one kind (hydrogen) that somehow keep "appearing" (God knows from where), and that get more and more complicated as they get together until they end up as stars and planets and plants and everything. The other starts with one mass of a simple basic substance, called YLEM for some reason, that explodes so hard it starts the whole universe off and also winds up as stars and planets, etc.

The purpose of this discussion is to point out that a solution of a problem by a mode of being that is irrelevant to the problem, where the data comes from a different construction of reality from that of the solution, is going to lead you, at best, into all kinds of contradictions and to false conclusions. In our example just given, a solution by the sensory mode leads you to conclusions opposite to those given by the clairvoyant mode. It is, at least by our best judgment today, the clairvoyant mode that is applicable to the problem.

A similar confusion has widely arisen in quite a different area. In this one, data has arisen from the use of the clairvoyant modes of being. Since, however, these modes are not generally recognized as valid, the interpretation has been made in the sensory modes or in a confused

contradiction of the two. This problem arises in connection with certain ESP occurrences.

The data includes occurrences of the type given earlier.
From the viewpoint of the sensory reality it is impossible,
yet it exists. People sometimes clearly show that they
have information that they could only have attained by a
violation of the basic limiting principles of the sensory
reality. From this viewpoint, the only viewpoint generally believed valid, they have done something they could
not have done, something clearly beyond their ability.
The obvious conclusion has been that it was done by
someone or something else who or that did have the
ability. Since human beings do not, these other beings
were—in this line of reasoning—not human. Therefore,
there had to be another class of intelligent beings around
who sometimes communicated information to people and
"told" them things they could not know through their
senses, or figure out from previous information they did
get through their senses. It seemed logically proven that
this other intelligent, self-willed, life class exists on the
planet with us. The only question was, Who or what are
they?

The usual answer in Greek, Roman, and earlier civilizations was that they were "Gods." This got rid of the
problem as to how this other life class violated the laws of
(the sensory) reality, as "Gods" can do this with impunity
and if you ask too many questions about "how," you are
clearly a heretic and need a spear down your throat. After
the Christian religion became the major one in the Western world, the concept of Gods became unpopular. For a
while the cultural decision was that it was either "God"
or "the Devil," depending on your relationship with the

local establishment. After a while, however, this choice ran into a lot of cultural difficulties, and the parts of the culture that regarded the problem as of any real interest opted for "spirits."

At this point we must proceed with caution and with a weather eye on our own biases. We must not judge this concept on the basis of its worst examples and devotees, but of its best. There is no question but that the majority of people who are using the spirit hypothesis in our culture are using it in silly and invalid ways. Their approach and evaluation are sloppy at best and schizophrenic at worst. Taking a legend from Plato that seems now to pretty clearly refer to the earthquake and tidal wave that destroyed ancient Crete, and from this legend communicating with dozens of spirit guides from Atlantis does not deserve much serious consideration. The idiot American Indian Spirit Guides of a half-century ago are in much the same class. This kind of data we can reasonably dismiss as "naïve" and "sweet," but this does not mean we can dismiss the entire concept. In novelty stores today you can buy "x-ray glasses" that are advertised to enable men to look through women's clothes and see them as if they were naked. These glasses do sell. This does not mean, however, that x-rays are not a legitimate phenomenon. We have to look at the data on which the concept of spirits rests and see if it is a valid one.

These spirits were—and are—generally regarded as ex-human beings who sort of hang around and sometimes communicate information. Very few people ask *how* the spirits get the information, even when it is precognitive; that is, it concerns future events that cannot be predicted from presently anywhere available knowledge. That is, how can the spirit violate the laws of (the sensory) reality? Asking it no longer, of course, gets you stuck with a spear, it simply makes you unpopular in these circles. (I speak here from experience!)

The number of persons who believe in "spirits," "spirit controls," etc., is very large and includes some serious and intelligent people; and the evidence, when you are actually working with a good psychic, can be very convincing emotionally. For a variety of reasons, the psychic usually is deeply convinced of the truth of the idea that she (most, but not all of the greatest psychics in our culture have been women) is communicating with a spirit, and this ring of conviction in her voice sounds like the ring of truth. Further, you are often being told information that you *know* the psychic cannot possibly know and it must come from somewhere. Humans couldn't know it under the circumstances, so it must come from nonhuman sources. With our cultural background, we tend to emotionally rule out nonhuman sources, but spirits least of all. So there you are: Spirits exist.

The reasons the psychic tends to sincerely believe in spirits are complex. Mainly, she is constantly faced with a very uncomfortable dilemma. She has clear, concrete information that it is impossible for her to have. It is very upsetting to be in a situation such as this with things happening to us that we not only do not understand, but that seem to be impossible. To put it mildly, it creates a lot of anxiety.[92] Automatically, there is an exploration of cultural resources for a solution to the problem. What has the society you are in to offer as a way out? The psychic finds that there is a large section of Western culture that has a ready-made solution. This is that spirits tell her the information. Since the pressure to escape the problem is very strong and the solution ready-made, presently the psychic begins to "feel the presence" of the spirits. Then it frequently goes even further and they are "seen" or "heard." If we need to see or hear something badly enough and are repeatedly told it is there, we are quite likely to see or hear it. Once the spirits are actually hallucinated, the conviction of their reality is overwhelming. It takes a very unusual psychic not to be completely convinced.

For many years, I worked closely with such an unusual psychic, Eileen Garrett, who was tremendously talented in arriving at paranormally gained information. In addition, she devoted her high intelligence and strong personality for nearly fifty years to trying to understand her own abilities. For the last thirty years of her life, she worked almost entirely under research conditions.

She frequently worked in trance; that is, she would give herself certain mental and physical cues and appear to become unconscious for a short time. When consciousness seemed to return, her voice would sound quite different and she would identify herself as a spirit, one Uvani, who claimed he was an Arab who had been killed by a Turk in 1850. Uvani was a composed, friendly, intelligent persona who—judging from earlier transcripts I read of sessions with him—remained a consistent personality for over forty years. (I must admit I miss our conversations since Mrs. Garrett died.) If you wished to speak with another spirit you would ask Uvani, who would reply in a sentence that always blew my mind a little. "If you will wait a moment I will see if he is around." There would be a moment of silence and then either Uvani would report "him" as unavailable, or else Mrs. Garrett would begin to speak in a different voice pattern, identifying herself as the person to whom you wished to speak. After the session was over and Mrs. Garrett was using her usual voice and displaying her usual personality, she would have no conscious memory of the session.

I must emphasize the convincing nature of these events. Very often the new voice pattern would be recognized by those who knew the person they were purported to represent as identical with the voice and speech patterns of the person when they were alive. Mrs. Garrett would use pet names, refer to incidents known only to the sitter (the person she was holding the session for) and the dead person who Mrs. Garrett claimed now to be and so forth. The feeling of *really* talking to someone you had known when they are alive was often so strong it would curl your hair.

Mrs. Garrett, however, was not herself fully convinced. I remember one incident in which the sister and widow of a man came to see her. She had never met any of them (the relatives or the man, "Dr. X," himself) and had never even been in the city in which they lived. It was decided to do a trance session and presently Mrs. Garrett was talking in a voice pattern I had never heard before and doing the "remember when" bit with the two relatives. It ended with the sister holding Mrs. Garrett's right hand, the wife the left, and both absolutely convinced that they were talking to their dear departed. Later, when the session was over and the visitors had left, I commented on this to Mrs. Garrett. She said, "Never forget, Larry, that awake or in trance, I am a very good telepath and the stage lost a great actress in me."

Now, she had *not* been faking. She was simply pointing out the dilemma to me. A psychic can either give you information you can check or information you cannot. If you cannot check it (as "on the third level of the spirit world the flowers have a beautiful smell" or "in ancient Atlantis..."), forget it: it's just fun and games. If you can check it, this means it is available somewhere, either in someone's mind or recorded somewhere, and therefore is available to telepathy and clairvoyance, which we know exist. Given them, plus good unconscious ability to dramatize an event and imitate a voice pattern, there is no need for spirit intervention.

Mrs. Garrett herself was never certain one way or the other. Shortly before her death, I was talking to her and told her that I would be very interested in what she thought about her spirit controls after all these years of serious investigation. She became very thoughtful for a moment and then replied:

> I have to answer you in a way that seems light and frivolous, but it's really very serious. It's sort of as if on Monday, Wednesday, and Friday I think that maybe they're spirits as they claim to be. And it's sort of as if on Tuesday, Thursday, and Saturday I think that they are multiple personality split-offs of my own mind that I have devised to make my life easier. And it's sort of as if on Sundays I try not to think very much about the matter.

I have said that the problem of the psychic rests on the need to deal with information gained normally in the clairvoyant modes. Sometimes, however, there seems to be more than this to the problem. Sometimes there seem to be physical effects. Although many of the occurrences are fakes, there are times when tables at a "seance" do knock, rap, or tilt up on one leg, and it is not a fake. There is clear evidence of this occurring under laboratory conditions where we can rule out trickery. Usually using the "one rap for yes, two raps for no" system, the raps identify themselves as coming from a spirit.

Here physical effects, loud knocks, tables tilting up on one leg (or sometimes entirely lifting themselves in the air) do occur. Since we know it is not being done by the people sitting around the table with their fingertips just touching the top, it must be done by someone or something else. And the raps give the answer that it is a spirit. The evidence seems very clear.

However, let us look at a recent research project in this field, an experiment that is, in my opinion, one of the two or three most important experiments ever done in psychical research. It was done by A. R. G. Owen, a serious, exceptionally well-trained mathematician, geneticist, and parapsychologist. Owen decided to re-create the seance situations from which so much of our evidence in the past hundred years in this field has come. However, he added some variations. A group of eight people was assembled and, working together, made up the story of a ghost. It concerned "Philip," an aristocratic cavalier of King Charles's time, who fell in love with a Gypsy girl. His wife, finding out about this, brought charges of witchcraft against the girl and she was brought to trial. The cavalier was afraid to testify for her although he knew the charges to be false and she was condemned to death. He became despondent, depressed, and finally committed suicide. This is a fine tale and typical of so many of the stories of spirit-entities. It was a complete fabrication made up entirely by Owen's group.

The group then began regular sittings awaiting messages from the cavalier. They used the best modern knowledge of procedures to put themselves into the potentially most-likely-to-produce-results states of mind. Presently they began to get knocks and rappings from the table. Using the questioning method of "one rap for yes, two for no," they established relationships with the ghost of the cavalier they had invented. He (?) became a very strong spirit-entity, able to produce raps and table tiltings (up on one leg at a sharp angle) under full light conditions, and with any six of the eight participants there. Under the full light of flood lamps and with movie cameras grinding away, the table would tilt and rap. The cavalier told the entire story the group had constructed as his own history with one exception. Philip insists that he never loved the Gypsy girl, it was just a case of sexual attraction!

It seems clear from this that the individuals in the group learned to use their own personal abilities—in this case psychokinesis—and are playing out the story of the cavalier with their aid. Although we do not understand anything very much about a mode of being that includes psychokinetic ability, we do know that such abilities exist. Since it is forbidden by the laws of the sensory construction of reality, the abilities must either be potential in a new mode of being ("new" in the sense of not being one of the four I have earlier discussed) or else potential in a deeper understanding of the clairvoyant, transpsychic or mythic modes.

The Philip experiment—and I strongly recommend reading it entirely in Owen's fascinating book[93]—does indicate again the lack of need for the hypothesis that spirits exist and intervene in our lives. The evidence for the existence and action of spirits can be explained in simpler ways.

But we must not be too certain. There is certainly nothing in the basic limiting principles of the sensory reality that forbids the existence of another intelligent, self-willed, mostly invisible, life class on this planet. That there is no evidence for it could also mean that we are still misinterpreting the meaning of various occurrences. In any reality there is always still a lot to learn about what is in it and how it operates and, with the best will and dedication in the world, we can all make errors. A classic error of this sort is described in the notebooks of Joseph Lister, a nineteenth-century physician who devoted his life to improving medical care and, in particular, to learning how to prevent and control infection. A student pointed out to him a bottle of urine that had been cloudy with bacteria the day before. Now it was clear and there was a green scum on the top. Lister answered the question as to why the bacteria had died by saying that the green scum was a mold called *penicillium,* and that by covering the top of the bottle, it cut off the air supply and caused the bacteria to die from lack of oxygen. If he had made the correct interpretation, he could easily have made a broth of cultured penicillium mold to slosh into wounds, and thousands of lives would have been saved between that date and the time the antibacterial effect of penicillin was discovered so many years later.

We must each be cautious in making decisions on things that exist or do not exist. When I wrote earlier of the hypothesis of underground nocturnal pencil-sharpeners to solve our pencil shavings problem, we were pretty clear it was an unnecessary hypothesis. With spirits we are less certain. There is, however, no more need for the hypothesis that spirits exist and communicate with psychics than there is for the little green men who come up at night and grind up all the pencils in the pencil-sharpeners. We can explain all the data that seems to support the existence of spirits in a much simpler way: on the basis of human abilities we know exist.

The spirit idea seems to me to be a rather typical result of what happens when you try to explain data arising in one mode of being by the methods of another. The ESP attainment of information in the clairvoyant mode is normal. The psychic uses this mode of being without very much, if any, sensory mode understanding of what she is doing. Attempts at explanation are made in the sensory mode, the everyday construction of reality where they are impossible for human beings. Therefore nonhuman entities must have done the work.

The only way we know of, however, that the spirits could violate the laws of the sensory mode of being is for them to assume another, a different mode. Then they can get the paranormal information. We know, however, that human beings can do this themselves. We do not need the spirits to explain the data. They become a nice fictional dramatic device like Philip to make it easier to continue with our culturally accepted idea that there is only one valid mode of being: the sensory mode.

So far the conclusion is that there is no reason to believe that spirits exist and that the supposed evidence for them comes from attempting to explain, in the sensory mode of being, data that was obtained while in the clairvoyant (and possibly the psychokinetic) modes of being. This, however, is curiously unsatisfying and we have the strong sense that our answer is not complete; that it is true as far as it goes, but does not go far enough, that there is something more here. We shall have to search further.

Before proceeding, let us be clear exactly what we are talking about. In the general area of spirits, there are at least three questions that are usually mixed up. The first is, Does the human personality survive death? The second is, If there *is* survival, is it as spirits? The third is, in mediumistic situations, What *is* a spirit control? The third question as to the nature of a Uvani or a Philip, Are they *really* spirits or are they unconscious dramatizations or what? is the question we are now examining.

This is not a question to be too easily answered or too lightly ignored. The feeling of truth when sitting with a good psychic is too strong to be just disregarded. The fact that so many serious investigators have come to the conclusion that some mystery is hidden here, that it cannot be simply explained as telepathy and psychokinesis plus unconscious dramatics, cannot be quickly dismissed if we wish to continue our search with integrity instead of bias. The fact that these investigators, often after devoting many years to its study, could not come to a clear conclusion is, in itself, disturbing. In addition, there are a couple of curious incidents and a few inconsistencies that perhaps indicate we must go on.

We will, therefore, look a little further. In doing so, let us remember that crucial clues are often hidden in the apparently clearest and most simple parts of a problem; in the places we least expect them. "Where there is much light, there is much shadow," wrote Goethe. There is a famous story by Edgar Allan Poe, *The Purloined Letter*. In this story it was known that a man had very carefully hidden an important stolen letter somewhere in his apartment. The detectives searched very thoroughly under and inside everything—walls, furniture, and so forth. They could not find it. The reason it was invisible to them was that it was lying in plain sight, on the writing desk, where it was so clear to the searchers that it could not be that they could not see it.

Very often in science we have found ourselves dealing with similar situations. What we were looking for was in a place so obviously not a hiding place, so clear and simple that it could not be seen. Let us see if perhaps a similar difficulty is involved here. Let us look at the apparently clearest and simplest part of our statement that there is no reason to suppose that spirits exist. Exactly what, we will ask, do we mean by the word "exist"?

"Come now," is the immediate response. "Don't complicate things even more. You have made enough problems already. Either spirits exist or they don't exist. This is obvious. Why try to pretend it isn't?"

But is it? A particular blue Chevrolet car is going past my window as I write this. It is going at a particular velocity. When we say the car exists, we know what we mean. Does the velocity exist? If it doesn't, what are we talking about? If it does, do we mean the same thing when we say so as we do when we say the car exists? You can see, hear, touch—and sometimes smell—the car. You can say exactly where it is at any moment and how much space it takes up. Can you do these things with the velocity? The car has length, breadth, thickness. Has the velocity?[94]

We are dealing here with a problem far less simple than it looks. It is a problem with which philosophy has been struggling for many centuries, and with which theoretical physics has had to come to grips in this one. In fact, one of the advances that has made modern physics possible is the discovery of the complexity and difficulty of this problem.

One technique of the sensory mode of being that science has widely used is relevant here. The technique is to invent something that does not exist in the sense the blue Chevrolet does, but is useful to fill a particular need or to describe in a shorthand way a particular set of observations.[95] Once invented (conceptualized) it behaves in its own way and cannot be changed. It is self-determined in accord with the way it was invented and organized. It is very useful—absolutely essential in many fields—and while we are thinking about it or using it, it acts as if it exists in the usual sense. Whenever we are not thinking about it, it does not exist. It exists, we might well say from this, only in certain frames of reference, only in relation to a certain way of organizing our perceptions, only in a particular universe of discourse, only for a particular purpose. But within this—and only within this—it does exist. Its use or function can be described, we can give it a name or a symbol, but it has no length, breadth, or thickness. It cannot be photographed and no instrument will register it. It can violate the laws and basic limiting principles of the sensory reality with impunity if that is the way it was designed. It is real and yet it is not real. It exists and yet it doesn't.

There are other strange aspects of the things in this class. You can't break them down into parts. You can use them and do things with them, but you can't break them up to see separately the parts they are made of. Further, you can't really ask what these things are, but only what they enable you to do. A very strange class of things, indeed.

Let us take as an example of these strange things, the "point of observation" of a telescope. It is certainly "real" and "exists," but it has no length, breadth, or thickness. We aim the point of observation on a wall a mile away. It is very useful and we can learn a great deal about the wall. No instrument or conceivable instrument in the wall or monitoring it could pick up the point of observation. When no one is thinking about it or using it, it does not exist. It's not in space and time and—by the basic limiting principles of the sensory reality—this means that it does not exist.

Further, it can violate the laws of the sensory reality quite effectively. There is one law, a theorem, that we have developed from the axioms of the sensory modes of being: that nothing can travel faster than the speed of light. I aim the point of observation one way into the night sky and am looking at the star Sirius. I grow bored and swing it over to Polaris. In a second or two the point of observation has traveled hundreds of light years. It has traveled far faster than the speed of light.

It is not like the body of the telescope, the metal tube and glass lenses, that exists in many frames of reference and can be used for many purposes. You can hit a stubborn colleague over the head with it, or use it as a paperweight, or stand it on end and use it for a duckpin to bowl at. You can take it apart and mail the tube to a friend in London and the lenses to a friend in Moscow.

We will call the body of the telescope a structural

entity because it has structure and parts. Its structure clearly exists and will continue to exist whether or not anyone is perceiving it, and whether it is perceived as an optical instrument, a club, a paperweight, a duckpin, an example of a particular instrument-maker's art, a clue to the technology or sociology of a particular time and place, or as anything else you please.

The other class of things we are dealing with, such as the point of observation, we will call functional entities since they have only function, not structure. If you try to use it for something else than its original purpose, use it in another frame of reference, you will find that it's not there any more. It has only its function (although that may be more complex than you know at first and lead you down some unexpected streets) and that is what it is.

We thus have an example of two kinds of real things that exist in very different ways. One kind exists steadily whether or not anyone knows it is there. We have called these structural entities, and if someone puts one of them—our telescope, for example—in a closet and goes away and gets hit by a truck and no one in the world knows it is there, it stays on in the closet until either the house burns down or someone discovers it. The other kind of thing we have called functional entities and these are real and exist only insofar as someone is using them or thinking about them. They exist very sporadically. Obviously, when we say that a thing exists, we mean something quite different when we are talking of functional entities than when we are talking of structural entities.

Are there other examples of this strange kind of thing that we could use to clarify the situation a little? One of the most widely used is the square root of minus one. This is generally shown as $\sqrt{-1}$. This term is more simple than it looks at first. A square root just means a number that multiplied by itself (squared) will give a particular figure. Thus, two times two equals four. Two is the square root of four since, multiplied by itself, it gives four. If we write "$\sqrt{4}$" we mean "two," since the figure "$\sqrt{\ }$" means "square root of." Since three times three equals 9, then $3=\sqrt{9}$. Three equals the square root of nine.

The square root of something means a number that multiplied by itself gives us that something. Obviously, if there is no number that multiplied by itself gives us X, then there is no such thing as the square root of X. X does not exist.

The square root of minus one ($\sqrt{-1}$) is very useful in a wide variety of mathematical systems. It is widely used and important. So we ask, What is it? What number multiplied by itself gives us minus one?

We then find out that there is no such number. It has to be one, since one times one equals one and no other number will give one as the result of multiplying it by itself. But a number is either plus (+) or minus (-). Let's try all the possible combinations. Minus one (-1) times minus one (-1) = plus one (+1). (I could show why this is so, but take my word for it unless you have mathematical training. And if you do have this training, you already know.)

Plus one times plus one equals plus one. So there is no such number as $\sqrt{-1}$, the square root of minus one. No number, multiplied by itself, equals minus one. However, $\sqrt{-1}$ is widely used in mathematics, and much of the engineering that went into building the last airplane you rode in would have been impossible without it. Is it real, does it exist? It clearly exists and functions when the mathematician is using it. Outside of that, it doesn't. You may or may not be happy with this answer, but I'll wager it's the best one you are going to get.

Further, you can't break it down into parts. (The symbol for it you can, but not the square root of minus one.) You can't even ask, with any hope of getting an answer, what it is, just what it enables you to do.

(There is the story of the student in the philosophy class who, after a particularly difficult lecture, asked the professor, "Is then everything a paradox?" The professor thought awhile and answered, "Well, yes and no.")

A decimal point or any mathematical point also has all the characteristics of a functional entity. It has no length, breadth, or thickness. (The ink on the paper does, but that's just a visual sign to you that a mathematical point is at that place.) Therefore, it cannot exist in the way structural entities exist. Misplace one in your bank account and see what it does to the relationship between the bank, your financial situation, and yourself. Anything that can cause that much trouble must exist, mustn't it?

There is the story of the philosopher Wittgenstein who was asked what a mathematical point was, since it had no length, breadth, or thickness. He replied, "A mathematical point is a place to start an argument." In the answer he was demonstrating that it had a functional rather than a structural nature and that these two are quite different.

One philosopher (Bishop Berkeley) thought that all things were functional entities. He defined them pretty well but couldn't believe that there were any structural entities. He got in a rather bad logical bind, however, because of the fact that some things clearly stayed around when no one was thinking of them. You could be hit on the head by a falling roof tile, of which no one was aware. He solved this problem in a way of no particular relevance to the way we think today. He said that God was constantly thinking of these things and that that is why they stayed around. Since God was always thinking of them, they continued to exist. This led to the little rhyme that Ronald Knox made up about an Oxford undergraduate who was a follower of the good Bishop:

> "There was a young man who said, 'God,
> must find it unusually odd,
> when he sees that the tree
> continues to be
> when there's no one about in the Quad.'"

Presently the young man receives a letter:

> "'Dear Sir, it is you who are odd.
> *I* am always about in the Quad.
> And that's why the tree
> continues to be
> as observed by, yours faithfully, God.'"

It is clear that structural entities do exist. The blue Chevrolet we spoke of before is one of them and will continue to exist whether or not anyone is thinking of it at any particular moment. But functional entities also exist.

Let us sum up some of the characteristics of these functional entities:

1. They exist only when being thought of, only when being used. Only for a particular purpose.

2. They have no length, breadth, or thickness.
3. They have no parts.
4. They function consistently and with unwavering stubbornness according to the way they were conceptualized. You cannot change the definition or its implications at will.
5. They can violate the laws of the sensory reality with impunity if they are organized that way.
6. They can affect our behavior.
7. No instrument or conceivable instrument (cameras, etc.) can register a functional entity. (It can, however, pick up the sign or symbol we use for a functional entity as a camera will pick up the $\sqrt{-1}$ from this page.)
8. Asking what a functional entity *is* gets you nowhere. You can ask what it enables you to do.

Interestingly enough, there is another question you can't ask about functional entities. Not ask and reasonably hope for an answer. The question is, Does it exist or not? You can ask this question about structural entities. It was designed for them. The particular blue Chevrolet we spoke of either exists or it doesn't. You and I may disagree as to whether it does or not, but—at least in the sensory reality—there is a true answer. For functional entities, we can ask other questions but not this one. We can ask, What does it enable me to do? What are the implications for its use in the way it was conceptualized? You can get answers to these questions, but not to the question, Does it exist? This question is simply not designed for functional entities. If you ask, Does the $\sqrt{-1}$ exist? you are going to simply wander in semantic circles.

We see a somewhat similar situation in art. So long as we are looking at an artistic production as an artistic production, the true existence of the subject is irrelevant.[96] When we question its historical accuracy we are no longer looking at, say, a painting, but a historical document. If I say, when looking at the "Mona Lisa," "Is she real? Does she exist? Did a real person called Mona Lisa look like that?" I am likely to be told, "Don't be silly, it's a painting." I am being told that it's the wrong question; similarly, if I asked if Michelangelo's "David" implies the historical David existed or did not exist. We can ask of an artistic production, "Does it 'work'?" "Is it artistic?" "Does it move me?" not whether it is real, whether it exists. We ask only if it communicates as art. Sir Laurence Olivier doing Hamlet may do a tremendous masterpiece—he generally does— or may do a flop, but both are irrelevant to there having been a historical Hamlet and how close the production is to his historical life. When we look at Picasso's great painting of Guernica, we do not ask if it resembles the village of Guernica when it was being bombed, but only if it moves us.

Well, what has all this to do with the existence or nonexistence of spirits? What, if anything, has it to do with the nature of a Uvani or a Philip?

At one time a few years ago, a psychologist was doing a research project that involved a long series of interviews with Mrs. Garrett in trance. There had been many conversations between the psychologist and the Uvani persona. At the beginning of one of these, the psychologist asked Uvani a question he had never asked before. He asked, "How have you been since we last met?" Uvani, an otherwise invariably calm and self-possessed persona, became completely confused, stuttered (the only time I ever heard him do that), and was unable to answer the question. In fact, he could not seem to *understand* the question, although on various other occasions he had asked the psychologist how he had been since they last met, and seemed clearly capable of understanding both the implications of the questions and the answers.

On another occasion Rosalind Heywood told me of the time when she was interviewing Mrs. Garrett who was in trance and speaking as if she were "Abdul Latif," her second major spirit control. Mrs. Heywood is a very gifted psychic herself as well as one of the wisest and most widely learned people in psychical research. She decided to use her own, highly developed paranormal abilities to perceive "Abdul Latif." She said, "I put out my antennae and it seemed to me that he only existed for the subject under discussion."

In these two incidents we have clues that these spirit controls may not exist between the times they are being "used" by Mrs. Garrett, and that perhaps they exist only for a particular purpose. It begins to look as if, when dealing with spirit controls, we may be dealing with functional entities or, at least, that it might be fruitful to investigate them from this aspect.

We have certainly been unable to register a "spirit" instrumentally. (There are apparent examples of their modifying people's behavior so that raps and table tiltings were produced by psychokinesis. However, we must be clear exactly what we are talking about when we are discussing, say, Philip. We are talking about raps and table tiltings in certain sequences. That is all we can observe, record, or photograph. These are, we believe, due to psychokinesis. It is the sequence of these, the coding, that leads us to the concept, the description, the functional entity, Philip.)

I have written that a functional entity inexorably follows the logic and implications of the way it was organized. There is a curious aspect to the Philip story. With raps he told the entire story of his life exactly as the group had made it up, with one exception. He denied he had "loved" the Gypsy girl, and insisted it had only been a sexual attraction. We must ask, "Why the exception?"

The organization of Philip was as a cavalier noble of the time of King Charles. A persona of this kind would have a great deal of personal pride, insistence on privacy of real emotion, and denial of any of the "softer" emotions. Sexual attraction would be very acceptable, love would not. If Philip were to be consistent to his own organization, "he" would do exactly as he did in respect to his attraction to the Gypsy girl. A functional entity remains consistent to its original organization.

Let us examine the idea of Philip as a functional entity a little further. We certainly cannot analyze him into parts. (A major attempt to do this with the spirit controls of Eileen Garrett did not succeed.)[97] We cannot do with Philip as we did with the body of the telescope, examine the component parts separately. If we ask what Philip *is*, well, eighty years of intensive investigations on spirit controls with this question have gotten nowhere.

What does he enable us to *do*? This is a legitimate question for functional entities. In this case, sequences of raps and table tiltings are produced that, taken in sequence, identify a "being" named Philip. We have here, it seems, a clue to mediumship generally. We might well suspect that sometimes a repressed and unfulfilled part of a person, the part that would be satisfied by the use of the clairvoyant mode of being, organizes itself in a special manner. This is closely akin to the multiple personalities in one person we see occasionally in psychiatric practice. In these situations a psychologically repressed part of the personality organizes itself into a coherent personality. In mediumship, the repressed parts, including those that need satisfaction in the clairvoyant modes, organize themselves into a spirit control. You then have a multiple personality with paranormal abilities. It solves the need of the person for clairvoyant mode of expression. It frequently also solves various psychological (and sometimes financial) problems, the need for a valued sense of the self, to influence and relate to others, and so forth. This is often a pretty impressive battery of satisfactions.

The spirit control enables us to externalize and use paranormal information and abilities. It solves the problem of living with the idea that I have information whose source I do not know, and that I could not possibly have since I believe that the only valid reality is the sensory reality. It also enables me to use psychokinetic abilities in a way that does not cause my anxiety and unbelief to immediately block them.

If Philip is, as he seems to be, a functional entity, we come back to our original question, Does he exist? This, however, is one of the questions you cannot ask about a functional entity. It now becomes clear that the reason we have never been able, despite the extensive work by serious people, to answer the question, Do spirit controls exist? is because it is not a legitimate question. The correct question is, Does it work? Does it enable us to do something? Can we use it? We can no more validly ask if Philip exists than we could validly ask if Olivier's Hamlet really existed.

I must confess that when I look at the conclusion this exploration has reached, I feel as if I had been telling the timeworn joke about two old friends who meet on the street after a long separation. After a few minutes the first man says:

> "What's the matter with you? After so long a time you don't even ask me how I am."
> Second man: "How are you?"
> First man: "Don't ask!"

Nevertheless, there it is. And we are not alone in having come to this type of conclusion. Don't, for example, ask a theoretical physicist if an electron exists. Mostly you will get nothing but a headache, as you will if you ask an astronomer about gravity, a sociologist about a group, or a psychoanalyst about the unconscious. This is the wrong question for all of these. It's probably clearest with an electron, which has no parts, violates the laws of the sensory reality with ease, and does not even occupy a definite amount of space. It is, perhaps, easiest with electrons to see how we are in the same position with spirits as a good many other sciences are with their concepts, but you can also do it in these other sciences directly. All of them have important things they deal with and react to and to which the question, Does it exist? does not apply.

If we have learned any one thing from the modern philosophical study of language—from Santayana, Cassirer, Wittgenstein, Korzybski, and the others who have devoted so much brilliance to it—it is that if you ask a question that does not apply in the frame of reference you are using, you are going to wind up chasing your own tail. You are simply not going to get an answer.

Certain people in combination with certain situations produce phenomena that act consistently as if there were another type of intelligent being, a spirit control, behind them. The construct of this intelligent being is an example of a special class of things called functional entities. Their validity is determined by their usefulness, which can be evaluated. The question of existence or nonexistence does not apply to this class of things, but to another class called structural entities.

In our analysis of spirits, however, we cannot stop here and still be true to the main thrust of this book. Willy-nilly we must go further. What has been said so far on this subject appears to me to be valid, but the analysis is not yet complete.

Everything so far said about spirits in this chapter is from the viewpoint of the sensory realities. Even the basic problem of explaining information gained in the clair-voyant modes is treated as a problem of the sensory modes. It has seemed to me to be valid to do this because this is how the problem is generally approached: "How do we explain spirits in our everyday, common sense, frame of reference?" However, if we stopped our exploration here, we would be implicitly agreeing with the usual idea that the sensory modes are the true modes that show the true reality and that all others have, at best, an inferior quality. From the viewpoint of this usual idea, until you have explained something in the sensory reality, you have not really dealt with it, and once you have explained it in this way of construing reality, it is explained. It is the central theme of this book that this idea is a limited one and that we are ready today to go beyond it; that we can now see that each of the four classes of modes are equally valid and must be dealt with in their own terms. If we are not to lose our nerve at this junction in our exploration, we must ask if the spirit entity concept is valid in any of the other four general classes of ways of inventing-discovering reality.

We have seen that in the sensory modes, spirits are an invalid explanation of data gained in the clairvoyant modes and also, under certain conditions, functional entities that we create and about which we can ask, "What do they enable us to do?" but not, "Do they exist?" In the clairvoyant modes, spirits do not fulfill the requirements for existence. (See Chapter 12). They are an invalid concept in this set of modes. Too little is known about the transpsychic modes to speak with any authority to this problem, although I cannot see the possibility of, or relevance to, the concept of spirits in the transpsychic realities. However, the mythic modes are another story.

In the mythic modes, no difference exists between objective and subjective. Whatever *is,* is real. No substance, form, occupation of space or time is necessary for something for it to be a real thing. All that is necessary is that it must be conceived of and reacted to as part of a complex of entities and energies that interacts with other parts of the complex. It is plain that spirits, as usually conceived, fulfill these criteria. In the mythic modes, astrology and numerology are valid activities and spirits can exist.

This is in no way a "putdown," a negation, of the

validity of astrology, numerology, and spirits. They exist in the mythic modes just as validly as medicine, chemistry, and lawyers exist in the sensory modes. Further, the mythic modes are as essential to our well-being as the sensory modes are to our biological survival. The concept of spirits and their actual existence is valid in the mythic modes *and can be used for the purposes of these modes.* These purposes, as we have seen earlier, are important human purposes. It is, however, only within these domains that they can be validly used, not, as is so frequently done, as an explanatory or action system in the sensory modes.

Some Further Implications
of the Concept
of Multiple Realities
XIV

What are some of the other implications of this new
approach to reality, implications for our daily life, for the
everyday processes of relating to ourselves and to each
other, and to the general nature of which we are a part? I
would like here to discuss a few of these implications.

As I start to write this section, I find myself thinking
first of what exploration of this strange concept during
the last few years has meant to me personally. What effect
has it had on me? As over several long days I try to think
this through, it seems to me that it has changed me in three
overlapping and related ways: in my relations with myself,
my relations with others, and my relationship with the
universe I live in and of which I am a part.

As with most of us, I was brought up and trained to believe that there was a right way to be. This is the way a good, decent, valid, or what-have-you person would behave, feel, and think. If, I was taught, all human beings, all "men and women of good will," would know the truth, they would behave, feel, and think in this way. Deviations from it were error. Brought up in one time and place, these errors were interpreted as being due to "stupidity," or "bad character." Brought up in other times and places, they would be interpreted as being due to "sin," "immaturity," "willfulness," "neurosis," "ignorance," the "Devil," or other causes. Whatever the interpretation, the results were the same. There was perceived a "right way" to be and any human being should naturally feel, think, and behave in that way.

The trouble was, none of us did. Being human, we kept falling off the straight line on one side or the other. First, there was usually some problem in the definition of the "right way." Frequently, it was not fully clear exactly what it entailed. Often—for many of us—it was much clearer what we should *not* do than it was what we should do. Secondly, it was never clear why our feelings and thoughts did not, or could not be made to, fully conform to the way they should. They persisted in going off on their own rather than "naturally" staying on the straight and narrow, which, naturally, increased our feeling of something being wrong with us, and increased our guilt. And, finally, as I see now, no matter what the exact or inexact definition of *the* correct way was, it would have fit only a part of any human being and left parts of him or her unsatisfied and undernourished. Human beings are too wide and varied, too innerly rich and multicolored to ever fit a definition of one correct way to be for very long.

The end result of all this has been a sense (underlying or on the surface of consciousness) of inadequacy to be what we "should" be, and therefore, of guilt. For some this background music is stronger than it is for others, and— for all of us—it swells and recedes during different periods of our life. But it is there and colors our being. It is almost universal in human life, since every mode of being includes as a primary statement that it is the only real and right way and no one mode can satisfy all our needs.

When we finally realize that there is no one right way for a human being to feel, think, or act, but only ways that are appropriate to attaining our goals, the situation changes. It is true that valid ways of being are not unlimited in number, they must conform to the definition of "valid" we have discussed earlier. But, within this scope, we have a much larger range than we have ever used. And, more importantly, the entire emphasis of our thinking and of our self-evaluation has changed. It is much less guilt-provoking to be essentially oriented to working toward goals than it is to be essentially oriented to working toward attaining a way of being that you feel you "should naturally" have been in the first place. We understand that we may succeed or fail in attaining a goal and that no moral self-judgment follows on either of these. If we succeed, we go ahead to the next goal in our lifelong quest for fuller being. If we fail, we learn from it and try again or set another goal. But we do not, with this orientation, condemn ourselves for our failure to be what we "should be."

One psychologist said that the only truly obscene word in the English language was the word "should," used in this sense. The sense of "I should be other than what I am" inevitably brings guilt in its wake. When we change our basic orientation toward reality and stop using it, the entire color of our relationship with ourself also changes. No longer is this form of guilt in the picture. When it is no longer present, we find that we do not need it as a driving force in our lives. Our inner tendencies toward action, growth, becoming, emerge as much stronger and flow much more freely when they are not hampered by an orientation that there is a moral law as to what we should be and the consequent guilt that we are not. And one gets a great deal more of zest and enjoyment and growth out of life the closer you are to accepting, growing, and celebrating what you are rather than trying to be what you should be.

This shift in my evaluation of myself has been helped by the study of this concept of reality as something I both discover and invent. I know that I enjoy a much more comfortable and friendly relationship with myself than I ever did before.

Another area in which my relationships with myself have changed is that I now seek and enjoy more ways of being at home in the universe than I did in the past. Originally trained as a typical Westerner and as a scientist, that the intellectual understanding of reality, the sensory reality, was the only real, valid and truthful one, I relegated all other modes to a secondary position and left large areas of myself unfulfilled. I might engage in these other modes when I had finished my work for the day (done my duty by reality!) and they could be a rest, a preparation, or a relaxation. They were, however, in my view, distinctly secondary and often not very fulfilling. They could never completely nourish the other parts of myself since they *were* seen as secondary and inferior. It is only when a mode of being is known as fully valid that it completely satisfies our needs, our hunger for the part of ourselves it fulfills.

I still have a long way to go and never expect to complete the task of finding new areas of myself to live and learn from and enjoy. Life is, for me, a never-ending series of doors with fascinating possibilities of vistas beyond them, if I will take the time and energy to do the hard work of learning to go through them. Each door leads to a lifetime of opportunity for exploration, learning, and growth, and there are more doors than I can count and I constantly learn of new ones. I have worked to enter a few of these more fully in the last few years and each has enriched my life and fed a previously undernourished part of me. Through the hard self-discipline of meditation (stricter than anything I ever experienced from the outside in five years in the Army), I have learned that I can move into a mode of being where I am one with the total universe and *know* that I can never be cut off from it. I can understand Giordano Bruno's statement, "Out of this world we cannot fall," or Suzuki Roshi, who put it "All is God and there is no God," or the Eastern mystic who meets all things and beings with the statement, *Tat tvam asi* (that art thou). I know that a part of me has needed and is watered and fed by the experience of being one with the All and that this is as valid and true a way of construing myself and the universe as the construction presented by my senses in the reality I was raised in; *as* valid and true, no more, no less. Neither *is* reality, both are exactly equally real ways of being at home in the cosmos, of inventing-discovering it. Both are truth, neither is *the* truth. Each serves and makes possible certain goals, defines others as "nonexistent" and "unreal." The combination of having both has certainly increased my zest for life, my productiveness, my serenity.

From music I have learned another way of being at home in the universe. To be able to listen *completely* without being aware of anything else for a time has nourished another part of me. It is not a part I can describe much in the words that were designed to deal with the sensory model of reality, but it is a rich part that is helping me grow toward a larger myself. It is a beautiful, strong, and often frightening path, filled with periods of feeling I can experience but not verbalize. As with all modes of being I am only at the beginning, but immensely fed by even putting one foot on the path with a whole heart. I have had a glimpse of what Beethoven's Waldstein Sonata played by Kurt Appelbaum can mean to me and look forward with eagerness and some anxiety to more fully experiencing it.

I have begun to learn (in my forties and fifties) the joy of fully experiencing my body and the organization of reality that has the focus of pure physical movement and action. Using such diverse paths as a school of body training known as Sensory Awareness, playing four-wall handball, taking self-defense courses, and lately the discipline of swimming laps in a pool an hour each day, I have begun to move in a direction new to me. I look forward to my first lesson in dance movement with the Noyes School of Movement scheduled for one week from the day I write this.

There are no limits to how deeply we can explore and live. If we would garden ourselves as completely as possible, we must search for and nourish as many parts of ourselves as we can. And we must know that there are more, yet unknown. The great Catholic mystic, Meister Eckhardt, put it beautifully five centuries ago when he wrote:

> There is no stopping place in this life—no, nor was there ever one for any man, no matter how far along his way he'd gone. This above all then, be ready at all times for the gifts of God, and always for new ones.

The second aspect of the changes that this exploration of the nature of reality has brought about in me is in the area of my relationships with others.

So many of our interpersonal problems—our pain, anger, and anguish with each other—have been largely a product of our belief in a right way to be rather than in exploring the goals we have and how best to reach them. Has there ever been a real difference in the *goals* of Catholicism, Protestantism, or Judaism? Clearly not, and yet there has been century after century of bitter conflict and uncounted dead and wounded in the strife between them. Each said, "There is a right way to be for all humans and the right way is ours."

Nor is there an important difference in the basic *goals* of. Russian "communism" and American "capitalism." One need only to compare the constitutions of the two states to see this. However, we have long since lost sight of these goals—if, indeed, we were ever very clear about them— and have concentrated on the different means we are using to achieve them. The bitter and long conflict between the United States and the USSR is not caused by a difference in what each is attempting to achieve for its citizens, but by a difference in viewpoint as to which system is the right one. As with religious conflicts, this orientation leads to conflict and battle. It becomes a moral difference. If, however, we shift to the problem of which way best achieves our goals, we may differ or agree, but the moral element drops out in favor of logical and scientific analysis. The "righteous anger" that makes differences almost impossible to reconcile is no longer in the picture. Imagine, if you will, two international conferences between the two nations. One is oriented, as have been all past ones, to the questions of whether capitalism or communism is right and which system shall triumph over the other. The second conference is oriented to the questions of the exact goals of each state for its citizens and the best way to attain these goals. The differences between the feelings engendered among the participants in these two conferences—and among those who follow them in the newspapers, radio, and TV—would be very great. The first has the air of a religious council deciding which of its members are true believers and which are heretics. The second conference has the air of a scientific group of specialists trying to solve a research problem. There are disagreements in both, but the second conference can ultimately decide them by scientific means and by recourse to research methods. The first conference can only decide them by implicit or explicit force. The question asked implies not only the answer, but also the way the answer can be found. When we concentrate on means alone, instead of goals and the means relevant to them, we ask questions that can only be decided on grounds of faith and force.

In terms of the history of societies, goals and means tend to go through a sort of curious dance of the kind called in ballet a *pas de deux*. First the goals appear on the stage and then the means appear as a way of supporting and attaining them. Then the means does its solo and takes center stage. The goals reappear in a very tentative way. They have become secondary to the means and a sort of vague excuse and background for it. The goals have been switched from main dancer to supporting cast. The basic questions asked by the ballet have changed and, inexorably following, the possible ways of answering them have also changed.

I have been writing here of political and international problems, but the same factors apply in our individual relationships, one to the other. One thing I have learned from this exploration of reality is not to judge another's way of life except in terms of how it helps the person achieve his own goals. I wrote earlier of how I, like most of us, had been raised to believe that there was a right way to be and a right pattern to behavior and that deviance from it was wrong. As I grew up and went into training to be a psychotherapist, the therapy orientation I was trained in reinforced this view. The therapist knew in advance which parts of the patient's life were "neurotic" and which were "healthy." He knew which parts had to be analyzed and which did not, which needed change, and which did not. The patient's goals in life were irrelevant. If they agreed with the analyst's goals, they were healthy. If they did not, they were neurotic. We were trained to adjust the patient to our own view of reality and to analyze him until he functioned in it. Whenever the patient disagreed with us, he was showing "resistance" and it was a sure sign that more analysis was needed in that area.

I paint a bleak picture of psychotherapy some thirty years ago, and although it is not entirely true,[98] it was the prevailing attitude and orientation among psychotherapists and psychotherapy training centers at that time. Few of us paid much attention to the wise psychotherapists who were the exceptions. When one of them, Karen Horney, tried to redefine psychotherapy as "a process in which you help another human being take his individuality, his 'neurosis' away from the front of his face where it acts as blinders, and move it around to the back of his neck where it acts as an outboard motor," we all thought it was a cute saying, repeated it at the next psychotherapy conference, and paid no further attention to it.

I believe I have learned from this research into our relations with reality to look at and relate to others differently. As a psychotherapist, I believe I now understand the meaning of Karen Horney's statement. I no longer see myself as a mechanic whose function it is to "adjust" my patients to reality and to "fix" what is wrong with them. I see myself, rather, as a gardener whose task it is to help each patient find out, so to speak, what kind of flower he is and, if he is a rhododendron, to become the best rhododendron possible, and to hell with what is popular in the seed catalogs this year; similarly, if he or she is an iris or an oak tree. Incidentally, I might add, psychotherapy is a lot more fun for both me and my patients since I made the shift to this viewpoint. It also tends to move much faster and my patients are interesting and fascinating people with more zest, verve, and style when they finish than when they started.

The change has been real in my functioning as a psychotherapist. In other areas of my relationships with others I have also learned not to respond to ways of life as right or wrong, good or bad, except in terms of how they help the person achieve his goals. I do not judge others except on this basis. What is sauce for the goose is *not* sauce for the gander, and one man's meat *is* another man's poison.

There is, for me, one exception to this. Where a way of life involves hurting other people or stunting their becoming, I believe it is wrong. It is based on inadequate understanding of the self and one's own goals. Whether one calls it neurosis, ignorance, or sin does not matter; it is adequately, for me, described by all three. It *never* is valid in any long-term sense; it always ultimately prevents a person from reaching his or her own long-term goals. Our basic nature is that of a being to whom good human relationships are as important in the long stretch as air, food, or water. Without it, a part of us is stunted; a basic part of the nourishment we need is not provided. The transpsychic modes of being fill a basic need of human beings, and unless these needs are fulfilled, we are stunted. The transpsychic modes contain, as a basic limiting principle, an ethical orientation, and unless we live it, we cannot satisfy these needs. "Do unto others..." is not an abstract moral principle, it is a necessary *human* guideline for our own sakes, our own being. If we do not live it, we do not escape unscathed. The slave owner is damaged by his actions; it is not only the slave who suffers.

But with this exception, I can openly and warmly accept almost any style of life in others, and I find that to the degree I can do this, I am enriched and learn from others. There are certainly individuals I do not particularly like, and some I actively dislike, but I feel under no obligation to like everyone. I can, now, however, accept their right to be their way and to follow their own path so long as they give me and others the same rights. Life has become a great deal easier, zestful, and more productive with this viewpoint.

I also find I waste a lot less of my energy in anger and recrimination. I do not mean to imply that I am less angry at injustice or phoniness. I'm not and I hope I never will be. Anyone who is not furious when a child is being hurt is an idiot who has renounced his or her membership in the human race. Anyone who says, "I am such an enlightened or wise person that I can see that *your* pain is illusion or unimportant," is a phony bastard. We need our anger against people like this, and against presidents who send out bombing planes to nurture their vanity or people who dump acid residues into rivers to increase their profits. There is no valid mode of being that, if understood in any depth, has activities such as these appropriate to its structure and goals. The infliction of pain ultimately brings pain for the inflictor, and "he who lives by the sword..." is true in all valid realities. Calmness and resignation in the face of injustice is for clams, not human beings.

However, outside of this kind of thing, I am finding myself much less angry at many of the different behaviors that in the past triggered my fury. Many of these—I see now—are appropriate responses to differents sets of goals and different structurings of reality from those I am personally related to. I can say to people I would previously have argued, and sometimes fought, with that I hope they fare well on their path, but I do not care to accompany them on it. I often regard their behavior as due to an inadequate understanding of the mode of being they are using, and may on occasion point this out to them, but so long as they are not harmful to others, I can wish them well. If a group wishes to sit around a table taking their guidance from the positions of the planets when they were born according to long-outdated astronomical charts, or listening to the Ouija board advice of ancient Atlanteans, that is fine with me, so long as they do not insist forcibly that I also follow the guidance and advice. I do believe that both these activities are the results of inadequate understanding of the construction of reality they are using, but I do not feel personally involved and therefore do not expend any energy on it. Very often the people who do these things are people I like very much and I can enjoy my relationships with them immensely. And often, to my surprise, learn from them how wrong I have been in my evaluation of their activities.

The third area in which exploration of the concept of reality described in this book has led to changes in my own life is that of my relationships with the general universe. It is a curious fact, noted in both schools of Western psychology and in the esoteric schools, that the more you heal the splits within yourself the more you heal the splits between yourself and the world you live in. To the degree we are alienated and cut off from parts of our being, from psychological, biological, and spiritual needs (these, of course, can never be separated for more than purposes of discussion and study), the more you feel cut off from the rest of the cosmos. The less you are at home with all of your needs, the less you are at home in the universe.

We can see this in what happens in those processes where we try to make ourselves coherent, try to help ourselves to function as one organism, responsive to *all* of itself, behaving with inner consistency. In the long work

of psychotherapy, we see that as we become more integrated within, we feel more integrally a part of the total
environment to which we relate. After the one-pointing
of disciplined meditation in which all our consciousness is
involved in doing one thing at a time, we find that we feel
a secure part of a total and unified Oneness that makes up
the All of being. (You can call it the One, God, the total
space-time fabric of the universe, the clairvoyant reality,
or Tao. Whatever you call it, the knowledge of being a
real part of it, and as inseparable from it as the note is from
the symphony, is the same.) In the intense, complete
absorption in music or the complete *being* of physical
activity or the total Oneness-of-being of intense passion,
the *knowledge* of being one with the environment and
cosmos is the same.

It is, apparently, the splits within the self that make for
the feeling of being split off from the rest of existence. As
this work I have been doing has progressed, my sense that I
am at home in the world has increased. The more I have
been becoming aware that I had needs that could not be
fully fed in the everyday construing of reality, and the
more I have realized that other modes of being were
equally valid, the more I have had a sense of Oneness with
nature, the All, or whatever I choose to call it.

Although the developments in my own relationships
and feelings I have described have made my life much
easier, more enjoyable, zestful, and productive, I feel only
at the very beginning of vast possibilities. There are a
tremendous number of things about which I am neuroti-
cally involved, unclear, ignorant, unknowingly or
knowingly prejudiced, afraid or confused, or any combi-

nation of these. I expect that this will always be so; the concept of "perfection" applied to human beings is a semantic disaster. I do hope, however, to keep on growing and becoming for the rest of my biological life. (After that, I'll see!) I know that this new concept of our both inventing and discovering reality can make new growth possible for both myself and others. How far it will enable us to go before it is outmoded and the next comprehension emerges is in the lap of the future.

Conclusions

XV

And now, perhaps, at the end of this long introduction to a concept of "what is," we can ask ourselves what sort of beings we are and what our relationship is to the rest of reality. Are we individuals moving separately, independently and with free will in an otherwise cause-effect universe in which the way of judging something is by whether or not it works? Yes, this is true. Are we all parts of the same ONE, as inseparable from everything else as is the sunlight from the air and this ONE a cosmos in which everything is as it should be as the total flows in full, predetermined harmony? Yes, this is true. Are we each connected to the great total of being, each separate,

215

but receiving our meaning and existence from our connection with the whole as a branch does from the trunk of
the tree? Do we live in a world of strong, clear, ethical
guidelines in which the good or evil, the growing or
stunting we do is also done to us? Yes, this is true. Are we
each a part of shifting webs of connection and meaning in
a world in which whatever is, is real and in which separate
things can become part of each other by an act of will and
in which everything is always unique, fresh, and exciting?
Yes, this is true.

Each of these realities is completely different from the
others and each is valid. We can embrace each one with a
full acceptance and enthusiasm, knowing each one serves
different purposes and needs, and that all are as equal to
our humanity as our brain, heart, lungs, and liver are to
our body. In doing and knowing this, we can nourish the
previously starved parts of ourselves so that we no longer
need in our deprivation and agony to turn our rage and
desperation on ourselves, our neighbors, and the general
nature in and by which we live.

Our freedom is so much greater than we have
comprehended. We can learn to shift from reality to
reality, choosing the one that is most relevant to our needs
and purposes at the moment, and use our new approach,
use what we are learning from the Kantian "revolution of
thought," to nourish our being, love, cherish, and garden
ourselves and each other, be at home in our universes and
help save ourselves and our planet.

Reference Notes

1. New York: Viking, 1974; Ballantine paperback, 1975.

2. "All theoretical concepts bear within themselves the character of 'instruments.' In the final analysis they are nothing but tools, which we have fashioned for the solution of specific tasks, and which must be continually refashioned." (Cassirer, E., *The Logic of the Humanities* [New Haven, Conn.: Yale University Press, 1960], p. 76.)

3. "Philosophy," wrote Kant, "is the attempt to answer these three questions."

4. This is a paraphrase of a statement made by Kant in his preface to the 2nd edition of *The Critique of Pure Reason.*

Elsewhere (*Prolegomena to Any Future Metaphysics*) he states, "The intellect does not derive its laws (a priori) from nature, but prescribes them to nature." This entire book can legitimately be viewed as an exploration of some of the implications and results of Kant's *Revolution of Thought.*

5. The philosopher Lotze.

6. This example is given by J. von Vexküll in his *Theoretical Biology* (London: Kegan Paul, Trench, Trubner, 1926).

7. "Just as the physical organism breaks up the matter which it receives, mixes it with its own juices and so makes it suitable for assimilation, so the psyche envelops the thing perceived with categories it has developed out of itself." (One of these categories is

217

logical thought.) (Vaihinger, H., *The Philosophy of "As If,"* C. K. Ogden, trans. [London: Kegan Paul, Trench, Trubner, 1924], p. 2) Henry Margenau has called this "epistemological feedback."

8. This phrase is from the mystic Evelyn Underhill, *Mysticism* (4th ed.; London: Methuen & Co., 1912, p. 24.)

9. These examples are from W. Kohler in his *The Place of Value in a World of Fact* (N.Y., Liveright, 1938).

10. "Indeed there are few things on which physics is so certain as that the properties of physical objects depend on the system of objects in which they are placed. What qualities are to be regarded as primary is simply a problem of logical economy, as to the smallest number that must be assumed such that all other properties can be derived from them." (Cohen, M. R., *Studies in Philosophy and Science* [New York: Harper and Row, 1949], p. 95.)

". . . There is no factuality . . . as an absolute . . . immutable datum; but what we call a fact is always theoretically oriented in some way, seen in regard to some . . . context and implicitly determined thereby. Theoretical elements do not somehow become added to a 'merely factual,' but they enter into the definition of the factual itself." (Cassirer, Ernst, *The Philosophy of Symbolic Forms,* Vol. 3, p. 143.)

It was Descartes who, for our modern age, pointed out in most detail that certain perceptions are so clear and self-evident that they are unquestionable and that any "attentive spirit" would agree on them and that they could be used as axioms. He included as examples $2 + 2 = 4$, $3 + 1 = 4$, $2 + 2 = 3 + 1$. (*Oeuvres,* Vol. 2.) "Any student of mathematics might nowadays refute the naïve intuitionism of Descartes by disputing the intuitive character of the propositions he used as examples. Descartes could not know that ordinary arithmetic is one among an infinity of conceivable arithmetical systems, including among others, the calculus used for counting hours and measuring angles, in which strange equalities, such as '$12 + 1 = 1$' and '$360 + 1 = 1$' are found. In alternative number systems—for instance those accepting negative numbers only—a proposition such as $2 + 2 = 4$ is not even meaningful, since such numbers simply do not exist in these contexts. Such noncanonical arithmetics may not seem 'intuitive' to those who are not used to them." (Bunge, M., *Intuition and Science* [Englewood Cliffs, N.J.: Prentice-Hall, 1962], p. 4.) In no way are these comments a questioning of the genius of Descartes nor of the tremendous contributions he made. What I am attempting to point out here is that *one aspect* of Descartes philosophy, which was of immense value to the period he lived and following ones, is now outmoded and, to the degree we keep it, hampers our arriving at solutions to our present problems.

11. The story was originally written by Voltaire.

12. This example is a slight paraphrase from Berger, P., B. Berger, and H. Kellner, *The Homeless Mind* (New York: Vintage-Random House, 1973), p. 13.

13. In his beautiful *Joseph* trilogy, Thomas Mann puts it: "The world hath many centres, one for each created being, and about each one lieth its own circle. Thou standest but half an ell from me, and yet about thee liest a universe whose centre I am not, but thou art... And I, on the other hand, stand in the centre of mine. For our universes are not far from each other so that they do not touch; rather hath God pushed them and interwoven them deep within each other."

14. This example is from C. E. Osgood, *Method and Theory in Experimental Psychology* (New York: Oxford University Press, 1953), p. 194.

15. "Before going farther it seems well to settle a question... Which of the numerous entities appearing on the scene of the present analysis are *real*, and which are not? As a physicist, this question holds no concern for me. In fact, I believe I should have very little interest in it if I were a philosopher. For there is absolutely nothing to be found in the part of epistemology needed as a basis for science, which would provide a criterion of reality. To assign reality only to what we have here called nature would be very arbitrary indeed and would, I think, offend the sensibilities of scientists severely. If, therefore, I were to define the realm of physical reality I would let it include nature plus all constructs which occur in physical theories held valid at present. To this realm I would also apply the name: physical universe.

"In the eyes of many, such a use of terms would appear to have two defects: First, reality would change as new discoveries are made and as new theories are developed. To deplore this would imply a desire to find *absolute* reality. But absolute reality is ultra-perceptory and hence is of no interest in science. For no amount of observation could ever verify absoluteness. The view here taken might be described as affirming *dynamic* or *constructive* reality, and I fail to see that it is even esthetically less satisfying than the postulate of an absolute, static reality. The physicist does not discover, he creates his universe." (Margenau, H., Metaphysical Elements in Physics, *Review of Modern Physics*, Vol. 13, No. 3, July 1941, pp. 176–189.)

"The philosopher C. S. Pierce pointed out that as human beings change, even 'Natural Law' will change. That these 'Natural Laws' are only observed regularities from the past and have no justification except experience. When our experience changes, the laws change. (Bury, J. D., *The Idea of Progress* [New York: Dover, 1955], p. 351.)

16. This example is from W. Köhler's *Gestalt Psychology* (New York: Horace Liveright, 1929), p. 328.

17. Unamuno in his *The Tragic Sense of Life* (New York: Dover, 1954).

18. "Neutral Monism" from Cohen, M. R., *Studies in Philosophy and Science* (New York: Harper and Row, 1949).

"This view is not so much a solution to the problem how the mental and the physical are to be distinguished, as a doctrine how the question must be put, in order to make the answer significant. It insists that every system, physical or mental, is but class or selection of neutral entities, and therefore can be defined only by the character of the fundamental principles or postulates of the system. The physical system is thus simply the class of entities to which our fundamental physical laws are applicable, and the psychological or mental system is the class of entities that meet certain other requirements, such as the capacity for specific response or what-not. Such classes need not be mutually exclusive, and their precise interrelation must be the object of specific detailed study. Thus, the whole physical system as an object known may be a single term in a mental series, while the mental series itself may be attributed to a particular physical organism in time and space.

"The question, How can the same entity be both in space and in consciousness? can be readily answered if we remember that the same thing can be in a number of different classes which are not mutually exclusive. A man may be in this room, in our association, and in a state of weariness, just as a man may be both a bankrupt and the author of a number of books on how to succeed in life.

"The assertion that the mental and the physical are complexes of neutral entities may suggest the question, Where and when do these neutral entities exist, if not in the mind or in physical space? The answer is that anything may be said to exist in a given universe of discourse if it can be shown that it occupies a position therein. Thus Hamlet's melancholy and reflective character exists in Shakespeare's play, and the roots of equations exist in the number system. For in each case the particular entity can be shown to be demanded by the character of the system and of the other entities in it. So far as logic is applicable to both physics and psychology, neutral logical entities may be said to be parts both of the mental and of the physical series. But insofar as logic is distinguished from physics and psychology, the system of logical entities exists just as truly as the mental or physical systems exist. In our daily routine, problems as to existence in the physical system are of tremendous concern, but there is no evidence for the view that existence in the physical or mental system is in any way logically superior to that in the purely logical or other system. This may seem to degrade the term existence, and perhaps it does. But I believe that few habits would be more useful to philosophy than the habit of refusing to discuss whether certain systems exist, unless we ask, exist how? or in what kind of system?"

19. Ernst Cassirer (in his *The Logic of the Humanities* [New York: Harper & Bros., 1946], p.|10) quotes Otto Liebmann:

"'Disbelief in miracles' is conceptually equivalent, or synonymous, with 'believing firmly in the absolute lawfulness of all events without exceptions.' It is to have *absolutely no doubt* as to the unconditional, objective, and universal principle of the causal principle: these two are simply equivalent concepts or synonymous."

When we are certain that a phenomenon such as firewalking *does not happen,* we are really saying: "My basic knowledge of how the universe works is so complete and so accurate that the cosmos holds no more surprises for me. I know all the real truths and the details will all fit them."

How sad, and how reminiscent, to know that someone feels this way. We all did when we were immature. (When we were "young" we knew better.) It feels familiar to hear this statement of certainty. I would wish this belief back for myself; it made a more comfortable world to live in. If only experience and life would not keep teaching most of us how little we know.

20. See for example Rosner, V. "Firewalking the Tribal Way," *Anthropos,* Vol. 61 (1961), pp. 177–190; Ebon, M. "Firewalking 1956," *Tomorrow,* Vol. 4, No. 4 (Summer 1956), pp. 71–73; Tenagras, Adm. A. "Firewalking in Modern Greece," *Tomorrow,* Vol. 4, No. 4 (Summer 1956), pp. 73–79.

21. Forwald, H., "A Study of PK in relation to Physical Conditions," *J. Parapsych.* XIX (1955), 133–154; and XXI (1957), 98–121.

McConnell, R. A., and H. Forwald, "PK Placements: 1. A Reexamination of the Forwald-Durham Experiment," *J. Parapsych.* XXXI (1967), 51–69.

Thouless, R. B., *From Anecdote to Experiment in Psychical Research* (London: Routledge and Kegan Paul, 1972).

Gibson, E., H. Gibson, and J. B. Rhine, "A Large Series of PK Tests," *J. Parapsych.* VII (1943), 228–237.

Pratt, J. G., and H. Forwald, "Confirmation of the PK Placement Effect," *J. Parapsych.* XXIII (1958), 1–19.

It is the parapsychologist W. E. Cox who more than any other person has studied psychokinesis and demonstrated its existence.

22. This is a paraphrase of a discussion by the physicist E. P. Wigner in his "The Place of Consciousness in Modern Physics," in Muses, C., and A. M. Young, eds., *Consciousness and Reality* (New York: Dutton, 1972), pp. 132–141.

On p. 136 Wigner goes on to say that if mind cannot affect matter it is the first example known in science where one system (here "matter) can affect another (here "mind") without being affected itself. We know that matter can affect mind (alcohol is one example). To suppose that the reverse is not true would be a strange anomaly. Interactions are two-way streets. There are, says Wigner, no one-way streets of this sort known to modern science or its theories.

23. Berger, P., *A Rumor of Angels* (New York: Doubleday, 1969), pp. 71 ff.

24. This illustration was suggested to me by James S. McDonnell.

25. This example is from W. Köhler's *Gestalt Psychology* (New York: Horace Liveright, 1929), p. 72.

26. This point is a paraphrase from Karl Pearson's *The Grammar of Science* (New York: Meridian Books, 1957).

27. A careful analysis of this is given by Jacob von Vexküll in his "A Stroll Through the Worlds of Animals and Men" in *Instinctive Behavior*, C. H. Schiller, trans. and ed. (New York: International Universities Press, 1957).

28. Werner, H., *The Comparative Psychology of Mental Development* (New York: International Universities Press, 1973), p. 339.

29. ". . . since all proof rests on assumptions it is vain for any philosophy to pretend to prove all of its material propositions. . . . We cannot explain experience or anything else without assuming something. . . ." (M. R. Cohen, *Studies in Philosophy and Science* [New York: Harper & Row, 1949], p. 10.

One of the great advances in mathematics occurred when the mathematician Kurt Gödel showed that *all* systems of mathematics must rest on a series of unprovable assumptions—"axioms."

30. The philosopher H. H. Price has described this "dualism," this

division of the world into what is "in here" (*res cogitans*) and "out there" (*res extensa*), as ". . . a very brilliant theory which has been very useful in the past, but is now a nuisance." Quoted in R. Heywood, *The Sixth Sense* (London: Pan Books, 1959), p. 224.

31. This is a restatement of a point made by Ludwig Wittgenstein in his *Tractatus Logico-Philosophicus.*

From Wittgenstein's *Tractatus:*

1.1   The world is the totality of facts, not of things.

2.1   We picture facts to ourselves.

2.12 A picture is a model of reality.

2.14 What constitutes a picture is that its elements are related to each other in a determinate way.

Anyone who learns a new language to the degree that they are thinking in it have by this action given themselves alternatives to the way they construe reality. Each language has some differences from others in the way it describes reality. Each has words defining things for which there is simply no equivalent in another language. The French word *elan* cannot be translated directly into English without undergoing some changes of meaning. Similarly, the Yiddish "Don't make me a tea kettle" (*Hoch mir nit a chinik*) suffers a major sea change when it is translated as "Don't make such a fuss about it." These (and the thousands of other examples that could be given) illustrate the slight differences in perception of reality that occur in languages as similar as these. Imagine then, the differences that occur between English and the tonal languages such as Chinese where meaning is based on tone as much as vowel and consonant differences. Or, to take this further, the differences in the indicated structure of the world between English and a computer language where all information is transmitted in different combinations of two indicators, "one" and "zero."

32. In particular, this has been pointed out by Ernst Cassirer in his *Language and Myth* (New York: Dover, 1953) and in his *The Philosophy of Symbolic Forms* (New Haven, Conn.: Yale Univ. Press, 1955).

A "culture" is defined by Cassirer as "Minds acting in cooperation through a similar definition of reality."

33. At least, as Suzanne Langer points out in her *Philosophy in a New Key* (New York: Mentor, 1962) a low opinion of *other* philosophers' metaphysics! Thus we have Bertrand Russell's "The belief that metaphysics has any bearing upon practical affairs is, to my mind, a proof of logical incapacity." (*Freedom Versus Organization* [New York: W. W. Norton, 1934], p. 196.)

34. "Seldom before," wrote Morris Rafael Cohen, "has the general craving for philosophic light seemed so vast and the offerings of professed philosophers so scant and unsubstantial." (*Reason and Nature* [New York: Harcourt Brace, 1931], p. viii.)

35. Some fascinating recent work in this field has developed from a concept of the philosopher Max Scheler. He coined the idea of a *sociology of knowledge,* a field of study devoted to the idea of how a culture develops and maintains a world view. Introduced to this country by Karl Mannheim, this field is one of the most rapidly developing ones in sociology and will, I believe, have profound effects in psychology, psychiatry, and anthropology. The best overall survey of it that I am aware of is *The Social Construction of Reality* by Peter Berger and Thomas Luckmann (Garden City, N.Y.: Doubleday, 1966).

36. This idea, that reality, the universe, etc., is orderly when looked at coherently from any level or angle, comes originally from the idea that God is rational. Therefore, His works would be rational and logically comprehensible. Despite (or because of or irrelevantly to) its origin in our culture, the idea appears to be valid at this time in our understanding. Future explorations may indicate other possibilities exist.

37. The most complete summary of this, the demonstration that any system being all in here or all out there, any complete empiricism or complete idealism, is bound to fail, was probably made by Edmund Husserl.

38. I first heard this example given by Alfred Korzybski in one of his seminars.

39. Aristotle gave this as the reason and it was accepted as valid for a very long time.

40. Heywood, R., *The Sixth Sense* (London: Pan Books, 1966), p. 175: "The most difficult mental act of all is to escape from prevailing doctrine."

41. This contrast between medieval and modern thought is a paraphrase of some comments of Morris Rafael Cohen in *Reason and Nature* (New York: Harcourt Brace, 1931).

42. This was the problem of the addition of velocities and other relativistic effects brought about by the Michelson-Morley experiments.

43. This example was suggested by Huston Smith in one of his lectures.

44. Von Vexküll, J., *A Stroll Through the Worlds of Animals and Men,*

pp. 12 and 30. In *Instinctive Behavior,* C. H. Schiller, trans. and ed. (New York: International University Press, 1957).

45. Sir Arthur Eddington.

46. This definition is one widely used in science today. In approximately this form I first came across it in W. Köhler's *The Place of Value in a World of Facts* (New York: Liveright, 1938).

47. Or, as Philip Wylie so aptly named them, "The City of Horror and Shame." and "The City of Naked Sorrow."

48. Quoted by Karl Pearson in his *The Grammar of Science,* (New York: Meridian, 1957), p. 272.

49. Ernst Cassirer, in particular, has pointed out that any meaningful definitions of man (or anything else) in terms of modern science must consist of discussion of functions, not of "what he is" but "what he does." Process has replaced static pictures in science today. This is explored particularly in his *Philosophy of Symbolic Forms.* In another place he wrote concerning this matter:

"Organic life exists only insofar as it evolves in time. It is not a thing but a process, a never-resting stream of events." (*An Essay on Man* [New Haven, Conn.: Yale University Press, 1966], p. 49.)

50. The sensory reality is the primary reality used by most cultures as it is the one geared to biological survival.

51. This sentence is from a talk given by Abraham Maslow.

52. The orientation of Western culture I have described can be seen illustrated (in both senses of the word) by book publishers. There are a very large number of books on how to *make* love, very few on what love is.

53. Bertrand Russell believed this to be the most significant discovery of the nineteenth century. (Cohen, M. R., *Studies in Philosophy and Science* [New York: Harper & Row, 1949], p. 112.)

54. "There is, in fact, no such thing as *the* form of the 'real' world; physics is one pattern which may be found in it, and 'appearance,' or the pattern of *things* with their qualities and characters, is another." (Langer, S., *Philosophy in a New Key* [New York: Mentor, 1962], p. 85.)

55. This version of the viewpoint was originally stated by the Roman mystic and philosopher Plotinus.

The poet and mystic William Blake prayed, "God keep us from single vision and Newton's sleep."

56. The ELEUSINIAN School. We have reason to believe that Plato's teacher, Socrates, trained in this school, and it is considered likely Plato did so, too. Plato certainly showed, in his writings, a very great familiarity with mystical principles and techniques.

57. Again I must refer to my *How to Meditate, A Guide to Self-Discovery* (Boston: Little, Brown, 1974; Ballantine paperback, 1975).

58. Items 9 and 10 are no longer accepted in modern science, which, especially the quantum theory, already transcends what I have called the sensory mode of being. Our general, "common sense" view of the world, and science, up to and including Bertrand Russell, would include these items.

Bertrand Russell lists the basic limiting principles of the sensory reality as follows:

1. The postulate of quasi-permanence.
2. The postulate of spatio-temporal continuity in causal lines.
3. The postulate of separable causal lines.
4. The postulate of the common causal origin of similar structures ranged about a center, or, more simply, the structural postulate.
5. The postulate of analogy.

Human Knowledge [London: George Allen and Unwin, 1948], p. 506.)

The philosopher C.D. Broad, in his *Religion, Philosophy and Psychical Research* (London: Routledge & Kegan Paul, 1953), defined them as:

1. The general principles of causation.
2. The limitation of the mind on matter.
3. The dependence of mind on brain.
4. The limitations on the ways of acquiring knowledge.

59. For example, "Euclid's geometry is...only applicable in a small region of space." (Heisenberg, W., *Philosophic Problems of Nuclear Science* [Greenwich, Conn.: Fawcett, 1942], p. 3.)

60. "...natural science contains no NORMATIVE principles dealing with ultimate goals; physical science is the quintessence of cognitive experience and not of values.... To know physical reality is to know where to look when something is wanted or needed to be seen; it is to be able to cure when a cure is desired, to kill when killing is intended. But natural science will never tell whether it is good or bad to look, to cure or to kill. It simply lacks the premise of an 'ought.'" (Margenau, H., *The Nature of Physical Reality* [New York: McGraw-Hill, 1950], p. 326.)

Although it is unfair to William James to tear one of his sentences out of context, he once summed up "right" and "wrong" from the viewpoint of the sensory modes of being:

"'The truth,' to put it very briefly, is only the expedient in the way of our thinking, just as 'the right' is only the expedient in the way of our acting." (*Essays in Pragmatism* [New York: Hafner, 1948], p. 145.)

61. "Nobody believes now that science *explains* anything; we all look upon it as a shorthand description, as an economy of thought." (Pearson, K., *The Grammar of Science* [New York: Meridian Books, 1957], p. xi.)

62. "The hope that new experiments will yet lead us back to objective events in time and space, or to absolute time, are about as well founded as the hope of discovering the end of the world [the jumping off place] somewhere in the unexplored regions of the Antarctic." (Heisenberg, W., *Philosophic Problems of Nuclear Science* [New York: Fawcett, 1966], p.19.)

63. "Doing" is always a contract between two actions, entities, thoughts, time periods, or spaces. When only one thing is filling the field of consciousness, there are no contracts, comparisons, or tensions *between*. We, then, are no longer "doing." We are "being." This is an entirely different state of consciousness from our everyday one and a completely different organization of reality.

64. *The Medium, the Mystic and the Physicist* (New York: Viking, 1974; Ballantine, 1975), pp. 99 ff.

65. New York: Simon and Schuster, 1966, p. 40.

66. *The Medium, the Mystic...*, pp. 253–277.

67. It is easy to dismiss these other views of reality because we personally do not perceive them. It is easy to ignore both the evidence and the clear testimony of some of the greatest of our race.

"...the parasites which live in the intestines of higher animals...do not need either to see or hear, and therefore for them the visible and the audible world does not exist, and if they possessed a certain degree of consciousness and took account of the fact that the animals at whose expense they live behaved in a world of sight and hearing, they would perhaps deem this belief to be due merely to the extravagance of its imagination." In M. Unamuno, *The Tragic Sense of Life* (New York: Dover, 1954).

68. In the philosophy ascribed to Hermes Trismegistus we find some of the clearest statements of the structure of the world under the mythic modes. In his *Asclepius* (one of his dialogues) he put it: "All things are connected to one another by mutual correspondence in a chain which extends from the lowest to the highest." His most famous statement of this (in *The Emerald Tablet*) was "As above, so below." (It is not certain that Hermes Trismegistus actually existed historically, but this body of writing is usually ascribed to him.)

69. Thus, in one period of time, myths were translated to be moral guidelines; in another, the way the primitive mind works; in another, a guide to how the unconscious functions.

70. "Creative thinking is thinking as a child with the tools of logical structuring given by maturity" (Michael Polanyi).

71. This idea, that play is the primary element of creativity, is far from new. So far as I know, it was first stated by F. Schiller.

72. The "play" element is universal in human culture. See, for example, Huizinga, J., *Homo Ludens—A Study of the Play Element in Culture* (Boston: Beacon Press, 1955).

73. This was first pointed out to me by Arthur Deikman, M.D.

74. The number of different general classes of modes of being that are valid for human beings is as yet unknown. Joseph Chilton Pearce, who has been exploring the area covered in this book (I recommend strongly his *The Crack in the Cosmic Egg* [New York: Julian Press, 1971] and *Exploring the Crack in the Cosmic Egg* [New York: Julian Press, 1974]), feels that the potential number is very great and perhaps infinite. I personally just do not know, although I believe the total number is small (not much above five or six, at any rate), rather than large.

75. This is a statement of the mystic de St. Martin. (White, A.E., *The Unknown Philosopher: Louis Claude de St. Martin* [New York: Rudolf Steiner Publications, 1970], p. 370.)

76. "Every saint is a man before he is a saint..." (Chesterton, G.K., *St. Thomas Aquinas* [New York: Image Books (Doubleday), 1956], p. 23.)

77. There is the story of the woman who was told that she had a fatal disease and went to have her portrait painted. She asked the artist to paint her wearing a magnificent diamond and ruby bracelet and necklace. When he asked her why she wanted him to do this when she did not own such jewelry, she replied, "After I die my husband will someday remarry. And I want the bastard to be really bugged by his new wife demanding to know why he won't give her the jewelry!"

78. A. Prince, W.F. *Noted Witnesses for Psychic Occurrences* (New Hyde Park, N.Y.: 1963), p.88.

B. Honorton, C., Ramsey, M. and Cabibbo, C. "Experimenter Effects in Extrasensory Perception," *J. Amer. Soc. for Psychical Research.* Vol. 69, No. 2 (April, 1975), pp. 135-150.

PG subjects obtained a significant (p = .02, 1-tailed) positive deviation from binomial expectation and NG subjects obtained a significant (p = .01,1-tailed) negative deviation. Subject means for the two groups (PG=103.72, NG=95.61) are significantly different (t=3.62, 34df, p = .001) and confirm the experimental hypothesis.

C. Musso, J.R., and Granero, M. "An ESP Drawing Experiment with a High Scoring Subject," *J. of Parapsychology.* 1973, Vol. 37, No. 1, pp. 13-36.
The agreement among judges in this experiment was high. The Concordance Coefficient, W=.69.

D. Prince, W.F. *Noted Witnesses for Psychic Occurrences* (New Hyde Park, N.Y.: 1963), p.33.

79. St. Augustine believed that there was no such thing as a miracle that violated natural laws. There were only events that violated our limited knowledge of natural laws.

80. *The Medium, The Mystic and the Physicist* (New York: Viking, 1974).

81. One mathematician, Kurt Gödel, pointed out that in relativity physics, which uses the clairvoyant reality, it is often impossible to say which of two events occurred first and which second. (In Schillp, P. A., ed., *Albert Einstein: Philosopher-Scientist* [New York: Harper and Row, 1959], p. 557.) In discussing this aspect of the clairvoyant reality, two other physicists, Lev Landau and B. Rumer, put it:

"[Modern physics has shown that] the words [that two events occurred] 'at one and the same time' turned out to be as meaningless as 'at one and the same place.'" (Landau, Lev, and B. Rumer, *(What Is Relativity?*, N. Kemmott, trans. [New York: Basic Books, 1960], p. 37.)

82. Curiously, modern science here has come full circle to the statement of Aquinas, "Everything that is received is received according to the nature of the recipient."

83. Dean Inge.

84. Ehrenwald, J., "Psi Phenomena and the Existential Shift," *J. Amer. Soc. Psychical Research.* Vol. 65, No. 2 (April 1971), pp. 162–172.

85. In Catholic philosophy this is known as the Theory of the Double Truth: ". . .a thing can be true in philosophy or according to reason and yet that its opposite can be true in theology and according to faith." (Copelston, F., S. J., *A History of Philosophy*, Vol. 2 [Westminster, Md.: Newcomen Press, 1957], p. 436.)

It is fascinating—and very much to the point of this book— to see how differently two different cultures see this theory. In the medieval period, all who espoused it agree that, when the two truths were in conflict, the truth as revealed in Scripture was the correct one, since it could not be in error, and the truth revealed by the senses came from the fallible senses of fallible man. In the modern period—well, let me quote from the physicist Werner Heisenberg:

"...two kinds of revelation of God. The one was written in the Bible and the other was to be found in the book of nature. The Holy Scripture had been written by man and was therefore subject to error, while nature was the immediate expression of God's intentions." ("Science and Culture," in *Science, Faith, and Man*, W. Warren Wagar, ed. [New York: Harper and Row, 1968], p. 23).

"In my observatory there is a telescope which condenses the light of a star on a film of sodium in a photo-electric cell. I rely on the classical theory to conduct the light through the lenses and focus it on the cell: then I switch on to the quantum theory to make the light fetch out electrons from the sodium film to be collected in an electrometer. If I happen to transpose the two theories, the quantum theory convinces me that the light will never get concentrated in the cell, and the classical theory shows that it is powerless to extract the electrons if it does get in. I have no logical reason for not using the theories this way round, only experience teaches me that I must not. Sir William Bragg was correct when he said that we use the Classical Theory on Mondays, Wednesdays and Fridays, and the Quantum Theory on Tuesdays, Thursdays and Saturdays." A. S. Eddington. Quoted by Tyrrell, G. N. M., *Grades of Significance* (London: Rider and Company, 1930), p. 56.

86. The concept of the survival of bodily death being up to the individual and what actions he takes is not new. Gurdjieff, for example (who founded an esoteric school in the 1920s), used to ask his followers, "Do you want to die like a man or perish like a dog?" in his attempts to motivate them to work on changing their consciousnesses. The concept is much older than this, however. It is also stated, for example, in Maimonedes' "Guide to the Perplexed."

87. In *The Medium, the Mystic and the Physicist*, and in "Human Survival of Biological Death," *Main Currents in Modern Thought*, Vol. 26 (Nov.–Dec. 1969), 35–57. The technical detail and references necessary to a full working out of these implications would, I believe, be out of place in the present book. They are, however, given in the above-referenced material.

88. "If the theory of relativity is correct, even in its special form, the meaning of independent particles is an absurdity because their states cannot be specified in principle." (Margenau, H., "Einstein's Conception of Reality" in P.A. Schillp, ed., *Albert Einstein: Philoso-*

pher-Scientist [New York: Harper and Row, 1959], p. 248.) We can legitimately paraphrase this quotation as follows: "If the theory of relativity is correct, even in its special form, the meaning of an independent I, bounded by special events such as birth or death, is an absurdity." Relativity theory is the mathematical approach to the clairvoyant reality.

89. The logical next question is, Which of my many moments of consciousness survives? Is it the consciousness of a moment of my childhood, my adolescence, adulthood, death? I have been many different self-aware, conscious personalities. Which one survives? The answer in this field is that the moment of consciousness in which you were most aware and at your highest level of being before death is the same one you are most aware of after death. The rules do not change with biological death, as this would indicate an illegitimate boundary line. Again, for the full details of the reasoning behind this answer, I must refer to note number 87.

90. This is not a toxic state nor is it one of despair or hopelessness. It is the true serenity and "joy" of the clairvoyant reality. Interestingly enough, there is frequently a good deal of the paranormal reception of information at this time.

91. Emerson wrote: "God offers men either repose or truth. Take your choice—you cannot have both."

92. The psychiatrist Kurt Goldstein called this kind of anxiety, the kind that arises when you are dealing with strong stimuli that have no meaning, that cannot be fitted into your comprehension of reality, catastrophic anxiety, and demonstrated that it was an exceptionally strong, painful, and ego-disrupting emotion.

93. Owen, I and Sparrow, M., *Conjuring Up Philip.* (New York: Harper and Row, 1976).

G.N.M. Tyrrell quotes Bernard Bosanquet "Everything is real so long as you do not take it for more than it is." (*Grades of Significance,* Rider and Co., London, 1930). In this fascinating book, Tyrrell struggles with and discusses many of the problems central to the present work.

94. "Take the questions, Is there a root to every equation? Is there a maximum velocity in the physical universe? Is there a special sex-determining factor in the germ cell? Did Moses have a real (historical) existence? Now in all these significant questions, the existence or non-existence of the entities in question is determined, in their respective sciences, not by reference to the question whether they are mental, but by reference to their relation to the body of propositions

which form the SCIENCE in question. What reason can there be for saying that roots and velocities have no existence, but that other entities do? Does it not seem that what we need is a fuller account of the different levels or types of existence?" (Cohen, M.R., *Studies in Philosophy and Science*, [New York: Harper and Row, 1969], p. 113).

95. In his intensive and extensive study of this phenomenon, the philosopher Hans Vaihinger has called these creations "fictions." (*The Philosophy of "As If,"* C. K. Ogden, trans. [London: Kegan Paul, Trench, Trubner, 1924.]

96. This point was originally made by Kant.

97. Ira Progoff, *The Image of an Oracle.* (New York: Garrett, 1964).

98. Followers of Alfred Adler, for example, were much less likely to follow this path than were those in the tradition of Freud and Jung. There were also some individual therapists who fought for the patient's right of self-determination and the freedom to choose his own goals and way. These included Abraham Meyerson, Harry Stack Sullivan, and Kurt Goldstein. They were in the minority, however, and were mostly voices crying in the wind.

DATE DUE

NOV 2 8 2000	